LEARNING ENGLISH

GREEN LINE NEW 5

Ausgabe für Bayern

WORKBOOK
mit Lösungen

von

Stephanie Ashford
Geraldine Greenhalgh
Rosemary Hellyer-Jones
Marion Horner

Ernst Klett Verlag
Stuttgart • Leipzig

One world

1 Aspects of globalisation (PB p. 8/ex. 1) *(Erwartungshorizont)*

a) How do these photos express different aspects of globalisation? Write your own captions for them.

1

2

3

4

1. *Jeans are worn almost everywhere in the world.*
2. *Football is played in all parts of the world.*
3. *The environment is in danger all over the world.*
4. *The internet connects people from different countries.*

b) Find photos and articles that show further examples of globalisation.
Start a class 'library' for the topic.

2 What are the words? (PB p. 9/ex. 2)

Put the missing words in the right place in the puzzle. (All the words are on pages 8 and 9 in your book.)

1. The ☐ industry produces and sells books.
2. A ☐ is a type of product that is sold under a certain name.
3. ☐ countries are countries in the third world.
4. Bad companies ☐ their workers.
5. The Japanese word for comics is ☐.
6. Some Chinese still ☐ goods on bikes.
7. Computers are examples of modern office ☐.
8. Having ☐ means being able to move around.
9. Companies want to make ☐ and become rich.
10. Modern technology helps news to ☐ fast.
11. With the internet we have ☐ to all kinds of information.
12. If you ☐ somebody, you try to be like them.
13. Our interests were very similar, so we had a lot in ☐ with each other.

				S	*D*		*A*			*P*	*E*	
M	*P*			*P*	*E*	*E*	*C*		*I*	*R*	*X*	*B*
A	*U*		*M*	*R*	*V*	*Q*	*C*	*T*	*M*	*O*	*P*	*R*
N	*B*	*C*	*O*	*E*	*E*	*U*	*E*	*R*	*I*	*F*	*L*	*A*
G	L	O	B	A	L	I	S	A	T	I	O	N
A	*I*	*M*	*I*	*D*	*O*	*P*	*S*	*N*	*A*	*T*	*I*	*D*
	S	*M*	*L*		*P*	*M*		*S*	*T*	*S*	*T*	
	H	*O*	*I*		*I*	*E*		*P*	*E*			
	I	*N*	*T*		*N*	*N*		*O*				
	N		*Y*		*G*	*T*		*R*				
	G							*T*				

3 Your message for the G8 leaders (PB p. 9/ex. 2)

a) Think of two or three things you would like to say to the G8 leaders.
Write down your ideas in note form in your exercise book.

b) Discuss in groups of four or five what you think the G8 leaders should talk about. Make a list of important topics for their next meeting.

⟨**c)**⟩ Write a letter to the G8 leaders. Use some of your ideas from **a)** and **b)**.

1 Talking about this and that (PB p. 11/ex. 3)

Write down what these people tell each other. Use the correct tense: ***simple past*** or ***present perfect***.

1. *A:* always want to try skateboarding – *B:* once break my leg in a skateboarding accident

   A: I've always wanted to *try skateboarding.*

   B: Be careful! I once broke *my leg in a skateboarding accident.*

2. *A:* buy a cool new mobile yesterday – *B:* have the same one for years

   A: *I bought a cool new mobile yesterday.*

   B: You're lucky. *I've had the same one for years.*

3. *A:* just hear about Madonna's new world tour – *B:* go to a concert of hers two years ago

   A: *I've just heard about Madonna's new world tour.*

   B: She's great, isn't she? *I went to a concert of hers two years ago.*

4. *A:* be a manga fan since last summer – *B:* never read a manga comic in my life

   A: *I've been a manga fan since last summer.*

   B: Really? *I've never read a manga comic in my life.*

2 In the news (PB p. 11/ex. 4)

Make sentences in the ***present perfect*** (***simple*** or ***progressive form***) with ***since*** or ***for***.

1. The G8 leaders are in Scotland. **(talk about world problems • early this morning)**

   They have been talking about *world problems since early this morning.*

2. It is a long meeting. **(already go on • hours)**

   It *has already been going on for hours.*

3. Outside lots of people are protesting. **(be there • the first leader arrived)**

   They have been there since the first leader arrived.

4. They are angry about the situation in the third world. **(get worse • many years now)**

   It has been getting worse for many years now.

5. A young German and a Scot are standing together. **(know each other • the last G8 meeting)**

   They have known each other since the last G8 meeting.

6. The police are there in great numbers. **(prepare for this event • many months)**

   They have been preparing for this event for many months.

3 A quick verb test (PB p. 11/ex. 4)

begin buy cost do feel hit know let light make

meet pay put run shut spell swim think win write

a) Write down the verbs where the ***infinitive***, the ***past form*** and the ***past participle*** are all the same.

cost, hit, let, put, shut

b) Write down the verbs where all three forms are different.

begin, do, know, swim, write

c) Find pairs of verbs with ***past participles*** that rhyme. Example: begin – do (begun – done)
(Use the list of irregular verbs at the back of your book to check your answers.)

buy – think (bought – thought), feel – spell (felt – spelt), hit – light (hit – lit),

meet – let (met – let), pay – make (paid – made), run – win (run – won)

4 Shocks and surprises (PB p. 11/ex. 5)

a) Imagine shocks or surprises in these situations. Make sentences with the ***past progressive*** for the background situation and the ***simple past*** for the action, and link the clauses with ***while*** or ***when***.
Use your exercise book. Example: 1. He was eating his hamburger when a girl on a skateboard suddenly shot past and grabbed it. *(Erwartungshorizont: S. 76)*

b) Think of shocks or surprises you have experienced. Tell your partner about them. Explain what you were doing at the time and what happened.

5 A world champion (PB p. 11/ex. 5)

Complete this newspaper article with the correct ***past tenses***.

A South African *has become* **(become)** the new world student 100 metres champion. Yesterday Sally Tambo *flew* **(fly)** back from Australia where she *had won* **(win)** the title two days earlier. "I *felt* **(feel)** great while I *was competing* **(compete)**. I *had* **(have)** a lot of confidence after all the good training I *had done* **(do)**, and that *was* **(be)** important," Sally *told* **(tell)** our reporter. "But I don't think I *'ve got* **(get)** used to the idea of being a world champion yet. I *haven't slept* **(not sleep)** at all for the last twenty-four hours. When I *arrived* **(arrive)** at the airport my family and friends *were waiting* **(wait)** to welcome me, and since then we *'ve been celebrating* **(celebrate)** my victory!"

An internet lifestyle

1 Teenagers around the world (PB p. 12/ex. 2) *(Erwartungshorizont: S. 76)*

What do teenagers around the world have in common? Think about their interests, likes and dislikes, dreams, problems, etc. Talk to your partner about your ideas. Use as many of the phrases from the box as you can. Example: *A:* Most teenagers enjoy hanging out with their mates.
B: Yes, not many kids are crazy about spending all their free time with their parents.

good at • (not) enjoy • interested in • imagine • worried about • dream of • (not) feel like • crazy about	+	**gerund**

2 Giving advice (PB p. 12/ex. 2) *(Erwartungshorizont)*

Complete the sentences with either ***gerund*** or ***infinitive constructions***. Use your own ideas for the advice.

1. How can I get the information I need for my geography project?

   You: I suggest *looking it up on the internet or in the library*.

2. I've got lots of old CDs I don't listen to any more.

   You: It might be possible for you *to sell them on the internet*.

3. My sister and I have arguments because we both want to use our computer at the same time.

   You: Have you thought of *making a computer timetable together*?

4. I hate exams – I always do so badly in them!

   You: Maybe you should revise instead of *reading comics all evening*.

5. I'm going to bid for a Geoff Rowley skateboard I've seen on eBay.

   You: You must remember *to be careful when you buy things online*.

6. A girl on the school bus keeps looking at me and I don't know why.

   You: She probably wants you *to talk to her*.

3 Food from another part of the world (PB p. 13/ex. 3) *(Lösung: S. 76)*

a) Put the ideas into an order that makes sense and write numbers in the boxes to show the order.

b) Write the full sentences down in the right order in your exercise book. Think carefully whether you should use ***gerund*** or ***infinitive constructions***.

- [3] I remember **(think)** how delicious it was.
- [6] I'm trying **(find)** a course that teaches authentic recipes.
- [8] Stop **(look)** so worried – I'll practise first!
- [1] I'll never forget **(taste)** Indian food for the first time.
- [7] I won't forget **(invite)** you for a meal.
- [4] Since then eating Indian food has meant **(go)** to a restaurant.
- [2] I'd stopped **(try)** it at an Asian street festival.
- [5] But now I mean **(learn)** to cook it myself.

4 The power of pop (PB p. 13/ex. 4)

realize • organize • help • get

enjoy • perform • persuade • listen • take

put • raise • see • treat • save

act • make • talk • prevent

Find the right group of verbs for each paragraph and complete the information with the correct constructions. Add ***prepositions*** before the ***gerunds*** where necessary.

1. Most people agree it is no use just *talking* about world problems. It is important for our leaders *to act* in order *to prevent* the deaths of 30,000 children across the world every day, even if this means *making* decisions which cost a lot of money.
2. Rock star Bob Geldof is most famous *for organizing* two huge global music events. He was the first *to realize* the power of pop music and the importance *of getting* the message across to young people that we all have a duty *to help* the poor of the world.
3. The aim of Live Aid in 1985 was *to raise* money for Africa. *Seeing* a TV report had made Geldof want *to save* lives there. With Live 8 in 2005 he was more interested in *putting* pressure on world leaders *to treat* developing countries fairly.
4. Geldof was so good *at persuading* other rock stars *to perform* for charity that sixty of the biggest names in the music business agreed *to take* part in Live Aid. Twenty years later fans were able *to enjoy* *listening* to the best bands in the world again!

5 Error spotting[1]: A comment on computers (PB p. 13/ex. 4)

Think whether the underlined words and phrases are correct or not. Look out for different types of errors. Use the lines below to correct the words where necessary. If there is no mistake, write the word 'correct'.

I use often [1] my computer and cannot imagine how I could [2] do many things so convenient [3] without it. It is especially useful for getting all kinds of informations [4]. However I do not want it to controll [5] my life. Some people are so use to doing [6] everything on their computer that they risk depending [7] on it too much. So instead [8] enjoying the advantages of modern technology they get [9] prisoners of it. A friend of me [10] often sits alone at his computer all day without seeing anybody [11]. If I would do [12] that I would go crazy.

1. *often use*	5. *to control*	9. *become*
2. *correct*	6. *used to doing*	10. *mine*
3. *conveniently*	7. *correct*	11. *correct*
4. *information*	8. *instead of*	12. *did*

[1] ['erə ˌspɒtɪŋ] – Fehler erkennen

6 Mediation: Using English as a common language (PB p. 13/ex. 5)

Imagine your class is replying to an internet message in English from a class in Beijing that is looking for friends in other parts of the world. Write down how you would express what everyone wants to say.

1. Sag, dass wir es toll fänden, Freunde in China zu haben.
2. Besteht die Möglichkeit, dass sie uns Fotos von ihrer Schule mailen?
3. Ich möchte wissen, welche Art von Musik junge Leute in China gern hören.
4. Möchten sie, dass wir alle ein paar Informationen über uns schreiben?
5. Frag auch, ob sie Interesse daran hätten, irgendwann mal Deutschland zu besuchen.
6. Sag, dass wir uns darauf freuen, bald von ihnen zu hören.

1. *We think it would be great to have friends in China.*
2. *Is there any chance of mailing us photos of your school?*
3. *What kind of music do young people in China enjoy listening to?*
4. *Would you like us all to write some information about ourselves?*
5. *Are you interested in visiting Germany?*
6. *We're looking forward to hearing from you soon.*

7 Mediation: What's that?! (PB p. 13/ex. 5) *(Erwartungshorizont: S. 76)*

Put the information under these photos into German for a friend who can't read English. Don't worry if you don't know every word. You will be able to explain the important points. Write in your exercise book.

A Japan's latest super-fast train has been seen for the first time – and it's got cat-like ears! The Fastech 360S travels at speeds of 360 kph and the ears on its roof help it to brake and therefore stop more quickly in an emergency. It is expected to be in service by 2011.

B A new restaurant has opened in Taiwan where you eat your meal while sitting on toilet-shaped seats! Other unique restaurants include a 'deaf' restaurant in Paris where you use sign language to order your food, and a 'blind' restaurant in London where you eat in complete darkness.

8 Mediation: Translating jokes (PB p. 13/ex. 5)

a) Work with a partner. Read these jokes and discuss whether they can be translated into German.
(Erwartungshorizont: S. 76)

b) Now think of one or two simple jokes you know in German and try to translate them into English. Does the joke 'work' in both languages?

"What did one wall say to the other wall? – I'll meet you at the corner."

"How do you make a jacket last? – You make the trousers first."

1 A newspaper article (PB p. 16/ex. 4)

a) Read the article once quickly to get the gist. Then go back and read it again more carefully. Mark the new words. If you can't guess them and you think they are important, look them up in a dictionary.

Young Spaniards turn to 'big bottle' drinking

From: The Sunday Times

The scene this weekend at La Viña del Señor, one of Barcelona's chicest bars, illustrated the relaxed drinking culture for which Spain is famous. Friends sat at tables and talked while they enjoyed a glass of wine in front of the Santa Maria del Mar church.

Appearances can give a false impression, however. Just a short walk away a gang of noisy teenagers were drinking from plastic bottles they had filled with whisky and cola in a ritual which is known as *el botellon* – or 'the big bottle'.

Gradually people in Spain are being forced to admit that alcoholism among the young is increasing. Drinking too much – which Spaniards have always seen as a problem of the British, Germans and other northern Europeans who arrive in their country every summer – is becoming more popular among their own young people.

In the past being seen drunk in the street was a matter of shame. Now *el botellon* has a positive image with the young and is spreading from Madrid to Barcelona and other cities.

"These kids don't have much money but they want to be rebellious," said Gema Lopez, a social worker in Barcelona. "Even sitting out in the street and drinking is something which shows this attitude."

A report by the Spanish health department found that the number of 15 to 19-year-old boys in Spain who regularly get drunk doubled from 22 percent to 44 percent between 2002 and 2004, with an increase from 10 percent to 24 percent among girls.

The Spanish government has introduced an educational programme to try and reduce alcohol consumption by school-age children. In Madrid, Barcelona and Toledo, people who drink in the streets risk fines of £1,000.

There are problems elsewhere in southern Europe. The number of Italian boys aged 14 to 17 who regularly drink too much increased by 31 percent between 1995 and 2000; the number of girls doing the same more than doubled. There have been increases in Portugal, too.

Sociologists blame the change in attitudes partly on the drinks industry, which has aimed its marketing of drinks at young people in southern Europe as well as in the north.

Derek Rutherford of Eurocare, a group that works to reduce alcohol-related illness, said: "The reason the gap is closing with northern countries is that we mix together more and are creating a common culture. The old wine industry has gone and been replaced by multinational drinks companies."

Spanish teenagers are beginning to imitate northern Europeans.

b) Complete the sentences to sum up what the article says. Try to express the information in your own words. (You may find this easier if you don't look at the article too often!) Write in your exercise book.

(Erwartungshorizont: S. 76)

1. Traditionally, drinking has not been a problem with Spanish teenagers, but now …
2. They do it because …
3. In order to reduce drinking by young people, the Spanish government …
4. The same problem as in Spain …
5. These changes have been partly caused by …
6. There is less difference between northern and southern Europeans than in the past because …

c) Discuss in groups of four or five the problem of young people who drink too much. Have you noticed this problem where you live or in places you have visited? Do you think there is a difference between northern and southern Europeans? Is it fair to blame the drinks industry for the problem?

⟨d)⟩ Write a comment of 80–100 words about why you think some young people drink too much and what should be done to try and stop the problem. Use your exercise book.

2 Listening: World news (PB p. 16/ex. 5)

a) Listen to some news stories and decide whether these statements are true (✔), false (✘) or if no information is given (–).

✔/✘/–	Statement
✔	1. There has been a disaster in Bangladesh.
–	2. Thousands of people have been drowned.
✔	3. Jobs will be lost in the banking industry.
✘	4. Older people prefer using the internet.
✘	5. Last year there were fewer street crimes.
✔	6. The figures in the report may not be correct.
–	7. World leaders have been meeting in Berlin.
✔	8. The meeting was not a success.
✘	9. American fashion shows are taking place this week.
✔	10. All kinds of colours will be worn next season.

b) Now correct the statements that are false. Use your exercise book.
(Erwartungshorizont: S. 76)

c) Listen to the news stories again. Then answer these questions in your exercise book.
(Erwartungshorizont: S. 76)

1. Who or what has already promised help for the disaster area in Bangladesh?
2. What does Oxfam say money is needed for?
3. What reason has Anglia Bank given for its decision?
4. What do trade unions say about jobs in banks?
5. Why are many street crimes not reported to the police?
6. What exactly have world leaders been discussing?
7. What are environment groups angry about?
8. What do most fashion designers' clothes have in common next season?

3 Cloze test: An Oxfam message about children at work (PB p. 16/ex. 5)

Complete the text. (Every seventh word is missing.)

In lots of developing countries children ___*work*___ in the fields or in factories. ___*They*___ are very often preferred to adults ___*because*___ they are cheaper. However, forcing companies ___*to*___ promise not to use children is ___*not*___ always a simple solution to the ___*problem*___. In many families children are the ___*only*___ ones with a job and so ___*without*___ their wages there would be no ___*money*___ for food. That is the reason ___*why*___ paying adults fairly is so important. ___*If*___ adults earn enough, then their children ___*needn't*___ work. Some companies have started to ___*realize/do*___ this.

So the next time you ___*buy*___ a product from the third world – ___*a*___ football from Pakistan or India, for ___*example*___ – check carefully that it was made ___*by*___ a Fair Trade company. Then there ___*is*___ less chance that you are helping ___*to*___ exploit a child in another part ___*of*___ the world.

Skills: Working on a project

1 Scanning a text (PB p. 18/ex. 4)

a) Imagine you are working on a project about the global home entertainment industry. Scan the internet text at the bottom of this page and mark the main information. Only look up words you can't guess if you think they are important.

b) With a partner, talk about what kind of information the text gives. Then go on to discuss what information the text does not give about the company. What other facts about it could you try to research? *(Erwartungshorizont: S. 76)*

2 Paraphrasing in your own words (PB p. 18/ex. 4) *(Lösung: S. 76)*

When you write your own texts, don't just copy from your sources. Often the style is not suitable anyway. Use the ideas on the right to rewrite these phrases in simple, clear language. Write in your exercise book.

1. Sony's roots were planted (line 1)
2. has led the field (line 7)
3. needed to regard the whole world as their marketplace (line 14)
4. developed into an international force (line 15)
5. took the industry by storm (line 26)
6. had advanced beyond existing formats (line 27)

- be the first
- invent a new product
- become a global company
- start
- sell products worldwide
- be a huge success

3 Organizing and presenting information (PB p. 18/ex. 4) *(Erwartungshorizont: S. 76)*

Look for important information you marked in the text about how the company has developed. Make a time line that shows the history of the company. Mark the important years and add notes about what happened in those years. Use your exercise book.

home

products

history

contact

Sony's roots were planted in a bombed out department store in Tokyo in 1946. Masaru Ibuka, an engineer, and Akio Morita, a physicist, started a company with 20 workers who repaired electrical equipment and built new products.

The success story really began when Tokyo Tsuchin Kogyo, as the company was named, obtained a licence in 1954 to make transistors. The transistor had been invented in America but it had not been used in radios. Sony made Japan's first transistor in May 1954 and the first all-transistor radio. Since then Sony has led the field in invention and innovation – with the first colour television in 1968, the world's first home use video system in 1975, the Walkman in 1979, an electronic camera in 1981, the world's first CD player in 1982, the first consumer camcorder in 1983, and so on and so on through to 1995 with the launch of PlayStation.

Since the company first began trading it has grown from 20 employees to over 100,000 people around the world. Morita recognized from the beginning that his company needed to regard the whole world as their marketplace, and not Japan alone. The company quickly developed into an international force. Sony Corporation of America was formed in 1960, Sony UK Limited was founded in 1968. Once products were being sold in a country it made sense to begin to manufacture them locally. A factory was established in San Diego in 1972, and this was followed by the factory in Bridgend to service the UK and Europe in 1974.

After its great success with hardware Sony has, in recent years, turned its attention to the software market, especially the production of software products that play on Sony hardware. In 1988 the company bought CBS Records to form Sony Music Entertainment, and in 1989 purchased Columbia Pictures to form Sony Pictures Entertainment.

The launch of PlayStation was the culmination of a long-term plan to take a lead in the video games market. It took the industry by storm. Sony had created its own games machine and had advanced beyond existing formats. It spent more than £300 million developing PlayStation and the investment has more than paid off.

1 Word power (PB p. 19/ex. 1)

a) Match the correct parts to make compound nouns.

sponsor • skate • feed • hand • dead • sports • over • high **+** rail • time • way • line • wear • ship • back • boarder

1. *sponsorship*
2. *skateboarder*
3. *feedback*
4. *handrail*
5. *deadline*
6. *sportswear*
7. *overtime*
8. *highway*

b) Write definitions of the words you made in **a)** in your exercise book. *(Erwartungshorizont: S. 76)*

2 At the skatepark (PB p. 19/ex. 2)

Complete what the people are saying. Choose from the verbs on the right and use ***gerund*** or ***infinitive constructions***.

not mean • forget • not remember • stop • go on **+** steal • practise • crash into • see • bring

1. "Oh no! I've forgotten *to bring my helmet*."
2. "Hey! *Stop stealing my crisps*."
3. "Sorry! *I didn't mean to crash into you*."
4. "Don't give up! *Just go on practising*."
5. "Hi! Are you new? *I don't remember seeing you here before*."

3 Mixed verb bag: The problem with new computer products (PB p. 19/ex. 3)

Complete the text with the correct form of the verbs.

Nobody *enjoys* **(enjoy)** *wasting* **(waste)** money, but a few months ago I *threw* **(throw)** away £50 by *buying* **(buy)** a new monitor. At the time I *was* **(be)** happy *to pay* **(pay)** for the latest product on the market – much better than the one I *had* *had* **(have)** before. However since then I *have found* **(find)** out that the same monitor now *costs* **(cost)** £50 less. I *noticed* **(notice)** the new price last week while I *was looking* **(look)** for something else in the shop – and *seeing* **(see)** it *made* **(make)** me mad, I can *tell* **(tell)** you! My own fault, of course – I should *have known* **(know)** that *waiting* **(wait)** for a while usually *means* **(mean)** *paying* **(pay)** a bit less for computer equipment. If only I *had stopped* **(stop)** *to think* **(think)**!

Tandem Activity 1

First find a partner. Then choose the left or the right side. Your partner takes the other side.
Don't look at your partner's side!
(Erwartungshorizont: S. 76)

A

Below there is a picture story, but three of the six pictures are missing, and the pictures are in the wrong order. First collect the missing information by asking your partner to describe his/her pictures and making notes. When you both know what is in all six pictures, decide together what the correct order should be. Then write the story in your exercise book (140–160 words). Choose the boy's name yourself and think of a good title for the story.

2

6

5

1

4

3

B

Below there is a picture story, but three of the six pictures are missing, and the pictures are in the wrong order. First collect the missing information by asking your partner to describe his/her pictures and making notes. When you both know what is in all six pictures, decide together what the correct order should be. Then write the story in your exercise book (140–160 words). Choose the boy's name yourself and think of a good title for the story.

2

6

5

1

4

3

Focus on technology and society

1 The Industrial Revolution puzzle (PB p. 21/ex. 2)

Use the clues to fill in the crossword. You can find most of the words on pages 20 and 21 of your book, but they might be in a different form there.

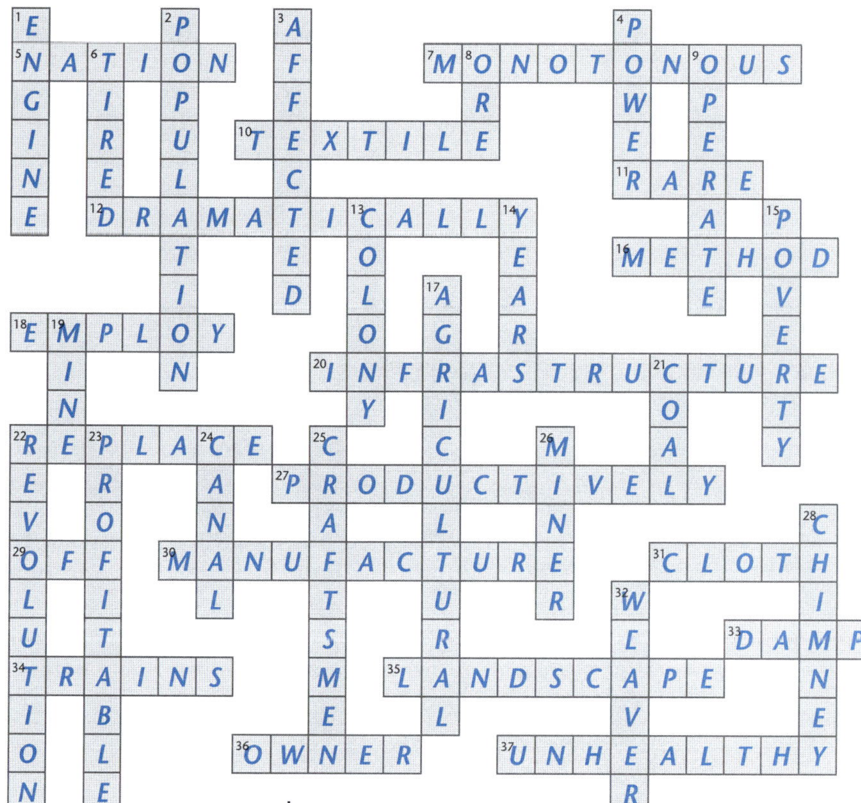

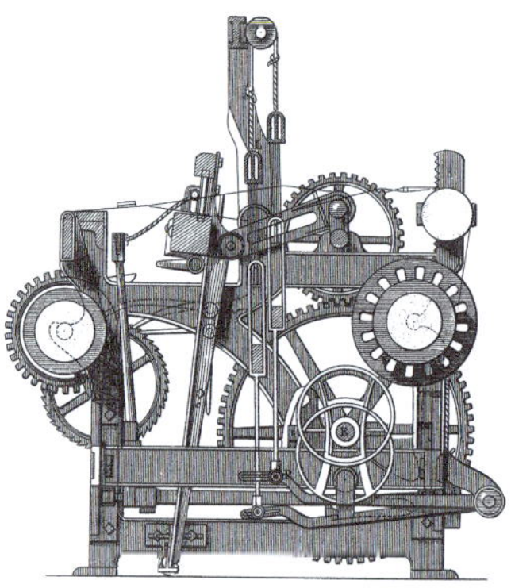

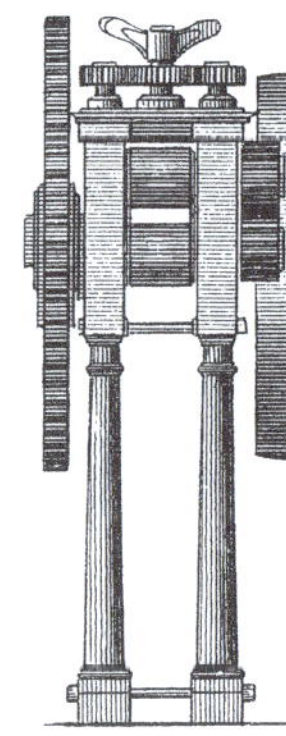

Across →

5. A community of people who share certain traditions and often speak the same language.
7. ☐ work is boring because you have to repeat the same thing again and again.
10. In the past, many women and children worked in ☐ factories.
11. A ☐ event is one that does not take place often.
12. Suddenly and quite amazingly.
16. The way you do something.
18. If you ☐ people, you give them work and pay them for it.
20. Basic systems of a country (for example, roads, water, power).
22. To take the place of something is to ☐ it.
27. A factory that produces a lot works ☐.
29. In the old days, some men took ☐ their clothes to work in the mines.
30. To make goods in a factory.
31. Textile factories make ☐ and clothes.
33. Slightly wet.
34. Steam ☐ made transport much faster.
35. Another word for 'scenery'.
36. If something is yours, you are its ☐.
37. Not good for your body or mind.

Down ↓

1. James Watt invented the steam ☐ in 1769.
2. All the people who live in an area or country.
3. Through the ages, new means of transport have ☐ the way people travel.
4. Today we often use electricity to ☐ machines.
6. If you worked from morning to night, you would feel very ☐.
8. During the Industrial Revolution, a lot of coal and iron ☐ came from the north of England.
9. To make a machine do its work, is to ☐ it.
13. A country or area that is ruled by a more powerful country.
14. The ☐ between 1750 and 1850 are known as the Industrial Revolution.
15. When you don't have enough money for food and clothing, you live in ☐.
17. Before the Industrial Revolution Britain was an ☐ society.
19. We get coal or gold from a ☐.
21. It is hard and black and you can burn it.
22. A huge change in ideas or ways of working or living.
23. If a business makes money, it is a ☐ business.
24. A kind of river that has been made to transport goods.
25. People who have the skills to make things with their hands.
26. Someone who works in a mine.
28. If you have an open fire in your house, the smoke goes through this.
32. A person who weaves to earn a living is a ☐.

2 Coal mines today (PB p. 23/ex. 3) *(Erwartungshorizont: S. 76)*

a) Read this text about coal mines and miners today. Compare the information here with the texts on pages 21 and 23 of your book and make notes in a table.

18th and 19th centuries	21st century
dangerous work, ...	mines safer, ...

Work in coal mines today is very different from how it was at the time of the Industrial Revolution. Safety rules and technology have dramatically improved the lives of miners.

There are many different kinds of machines which now remove the coal from the mine walls, hold up the roofs of the mines so that they don't collapse and then transport the coal quickly and efficiently out of the mine. Most of these machines are operated by computers. Fresh air from above consistently moves through the mine to get rid of dangerous gases and also helps to make the mine a less dusty environment. The miners wear hard hats, strong boots and special clothing to protect themselves.

Of course, all the miners have a good education and many have received special training courses. On average a miner today works about eight hours a day and earns a good income. However, a large number of coal mines in Britain have closed over the years, so many miners have lost their jobs and have found it difficult to find other work.

b) Now use your notes in **a)** to write a text which compares the life of a miner in the 18th and 19th centuries to the life of a miner today.

3 A friend for life? (PB p. 23/ex. 5)

a) Read this text from a website. Then discuss these questions with a partner and write your answers in your exercise book. *(Erwartungshorizont: S. 76)*

1. Would you like to have a robot like Aibo? Why or why not?
2. Do you think Aibo is a useful invention? Why or why not?
3. Can you think of different people who might find the idea of a robot dog attractive? Make a list of the reasons why.

home

Aibo

Have you ever felt that you need someone who is always there? Do you feel lonely when you're all by yourself? Are your parents against pets? Well, Aibo could be the answer! 'Aibo' means 'pal' in Japanese. This robot dog comes in gold, silver or black. Although Aibo is a robot, he is great company. He can move his tail and ears and he can even play games with you that no real dog could!

Aibo has a camera in his nose which you can operate. Just give the simple command "Take a picture!" and Aibo will take a photo of what he sees. Aibo can also recognize the voice of his owner, identify his own name and he can learn up to 40 words. He can express his feelings as well, so be careful how you treat him. Ignore him and he will become sad and won't talk.

Aibo costs a cool $2,300, but he could be a friend for life and that doesn't come cheap. The first 3,000 robot dogs were sold in 20 minutes and now the Japanese company plans to manufacture a version that would only cost $1,300. They believe that they will be able to produce 60,000 robot dogs a month.

⟨b)⟩ Think of an invention that you would find useful and write an advert for it in your exercise book. First explain what it is and what it can do. Then say which people would find it useful and why.

4 Best friends (PB p. 23/ex. 5)

a) What are these people talking about? Match the photos to the different people and write the correct numbers in the boxes.

[8] I've got a job in a factory and my work is pretty monotonous. I can't even talk to other people because the workshop is so noisy. It really helps me to survive the day.

[5] I think we would all be lost without it. I have to work all day, my husband always comes home late and the kids just come in when they're hungry. It's just so quick and easy.

[4] We live in North India and it's really changed our life a lot here. Now, my mother doesn't have to send me out to go shopping every day and she doesn't have to cook every mealtime. Even dad can get a cold beer at home.

[7] I can take it anywhere with me because it's so small. It even records directly onto a small CD. Now I can make my own top quality films. It's brilliant!

1

2

3

4

5
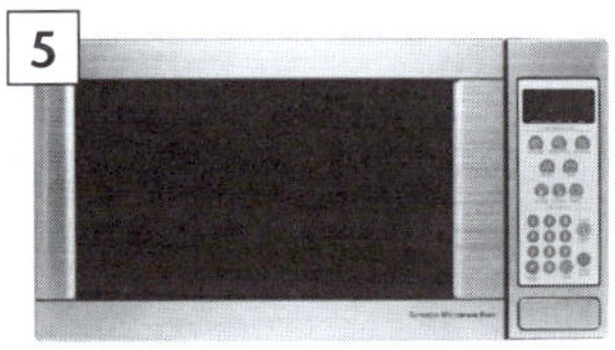
6

7
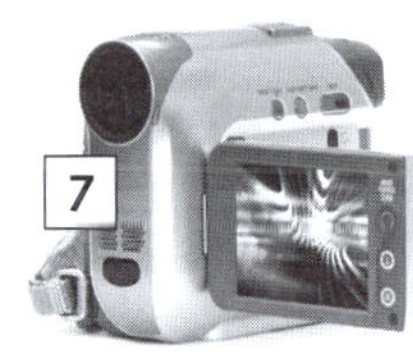
8
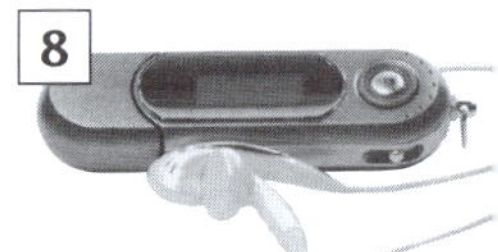

b) Name the things in the other photos and say what you use them for. *(Erwartungshorizont: S. 77)*

c) Which piece of technology is your best friend? Explain in your exercise book why, but don't say what it is. Then exchange your exercise book with a partner's and see if you can guess what it is.

5 Listening: Telephone technology (PB p. 23/ex. 6)

a) Listen to Ted on the phone and tick ✔ the correct boxes.

1. Ted calls the mobile number and
- [ ] a) he leaves a message.
- [ ] b) a voice says the person is busy.
- [x] c) he realizes the mobile has been switched off.

2. The office Ted phones is a
- [ ] a) company that makes blankets.
- [x] b) computer company.
- [ ] c) telephone company.

3. If Ted wants to talk to someone in the company, he should press
- [ ] a) three.
- [ ] b) two.
- [x] c) four.

4. Ted wants to talk to someone in the
- [x] a) customer department.
- [ ] b) information department.
- [ ] c) repairs workshop.

5. Ted would like to
- [ ] a) order something.
- [x] b) speak to his wife.
- [ ] c) listen to music.

6. Ted really
- [ ] a) likes the service.
- [x] b) feels angry.
- [ ] c) loves the music.

7. When Ted hears Mary's voice he is
- [x] a) very happy.
- [ ] b) disappointed.
- [ ] c) frightened.

8. Mary asks Ted
- [ ] a) what he thinks of the telephone system.
- [ ] b) to talk to an important customer.
- [x] c) to phone her later.

b) Write answers to these questions in your exercise book. *(Erwartungshorizont: S. 77)*

1. Have you ever been in a similar situation to Ted? If so, who did you want to talk to and how did you feel? If not, think of Ted and imagine how you would feel in his situation.
2. In what ways is or isn't this kind of telephone system a help? Think about both companies and customers. Give reasons and then compare them with a partner or in class.

unit 2 intro

From school to work

1 Listening: The right job (PB p. 25/ex. 2)

a) Judy sees Fiona and Nadim looking at the school notice board. They start talking about what to do after school. Listen and tick ✔ the right names.

Who …	Judy	Nadim	Fiona
• hasn't decided yet?	✔		✔
• doesn't want to go to college or university?			✔
• enjoys Arts subjects?			✔
• enjoys Science and Maths?		✔	
• needs to go to university for his/her career?		✔	
• wants to see the world before studying/working?			✔
• doesn't want to do what his/her parents want?		✔	✔
• enjoys doing practical things?	✔		✔
• would like to work with people?	✔		

b) What advice does Nadim think the person from the job centre will give pupils? *(Erwartungshorizont)*

Nadim thinks he or she will tell pupils to go to college or do a training course.

c) Suggest three jobs for Judy and explain why you think they would suit her. Write in your exercise book. *(Erwartungshorizont: S. 77)*

2 Word power (PB p. 25/ex. 4)

a) Match the verbs with the groups of nouns they can go with.

take **gain** **do** **have** **make**

1. *make* a mistake/a profit/money
2. *take* things apart/a year off/exams
3. *have* a degree[1]/a party/a baby
4. *gain* experience/an advantage/weight
5. *do* voluntary work/the shopping/Technology (at university)

b) Complete the sentences with suitable nouns from **a)**.

Nadim's parents don't want him to do *Technology* at university. They think it's better to have *a degree* in Management so that he can take over the family business. He has already gained a lot of *experience* from helping his dad. Fiona would like to take *a year off* to see the world. She can't do *voluntary work* for charity, because she needs to make some *money* while she is travelling. Judy would like to have *a baby* but she isn't ready to be a mother yet. Nadim, Fiona and Judy are taking *exams* next week and afterwards they'll have *a party* to celebrate.

c) Write your own sentences in your exercise book using the verb-noun pairs you did not use in **b)**. *(Erwartungshorizont: S. 77)*

⟨d)⟩ Find four more nouns to go with the verbs in **a)** and write your own sentences with them. Use your exercise book. *(Erwartungshorizont: S. 77)*

[1][dɪ'griː] – Universitätsabschluss

1 Everyday English: Let's go ice-skating (PB p. 26/ex. 2)

Look at the **marked** words and cross out the wrong ones.

1. *Nadim:* What ~~do you do~~/**are you doing** on Saturday, Fiona? Have you got any plans?
2. *Fiona:* Yes, **I'm going**/~~I go~~ shopping with my mum in the morning. **We're getting**/~~We get~~ some new curtains for my bedroom.
3. *Nadim:* ~~Would you like~~/**Do you fancy** coming ice-skating with me in the afternoon?
4. *Fiona:* I'd love to, but I **always have**/~~am always having~~ my dance class on Saturday afternoons.
5. *Nadim:* When **does your class finish**/~~is your class finishing~~? I could buy you a pizza.
6. *Fiona:* It's kind of you to invite me, but my class **lasts**/~~is lasting~~ from 5 pm to 7.30 pm, so I ~~probably am~~/**will probably be** too tired ~~after~~/**afterwards**.
7. *Nadim:* Well, would Sunday ~~fit~~/**suit** you better?
8. *Fiona:* Not really, Nadim, because ~~we move~~/**we're moving** to our new house on Sunday. Maybe we could **meet up**/~~meet us~~ to go ice-skating this evening instead.
9. *Nadim:* I'm **sorry**/~~afraid~~, but that won't be possible. ~~I see~~/**I'm seeing** someone else tonight.

4 2 Listening: What will they be doing? (PB p. 27/ex. 3)

a) First listen to the fortune teller[1] and put the pictures in the right order. Then listen again and put in the names of the people under the right pictures.

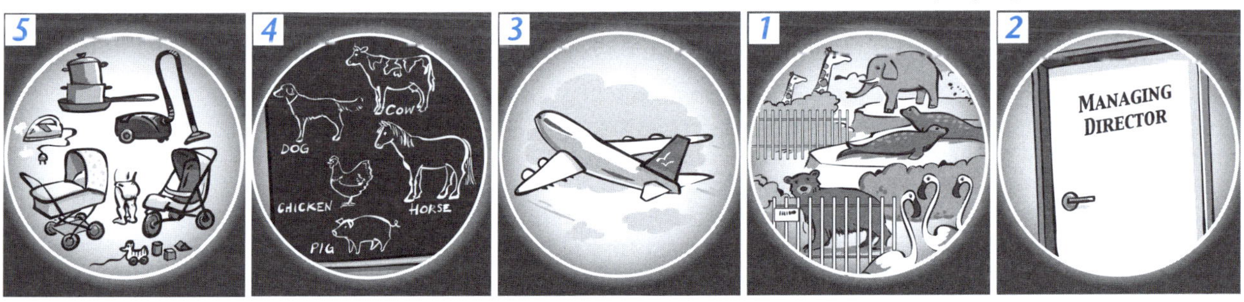

5	4	3	1	2
Judy	*Fiona*	*Nadim*	*Trish*	*Mike*

b) For each person, write two sentences about what they will or won't be doing in five years' time. Use each of the verbs in the box once.

care for • deal with • earn • fly • live • look after • run • serve • spend • teach

(Erwartungshorizont)

1. **Trish** *won't be dealing with pets.*
She will be looking after animals in a zoo.

2. **Mike** *will be running his own company.*
He won't be spending every weekend in the office.

3. **Nadim** *won't be serving meals and drinks to passengers.*
He will be flying a plane (himself) as a pilot.

4. **Fiona** *won't be living in Scotland.*
She will be teaching English to children.

5. **Judy** *won't be earning any money.*
She will be caring for her own three children.

[1] ['fɔːtʃuːn ˌtelə] – Wahrsagerin

3 Fiona's earrings (PB p. 27/ex. 4)

Fiona designs earrings and sells them to her friends. They are very popular and she can make an average of five pairs a day. Each pair costs £1 to make, but she sells them for £5. Rewrite the text with the verbs in the ***future perfect*** and add the missing information.

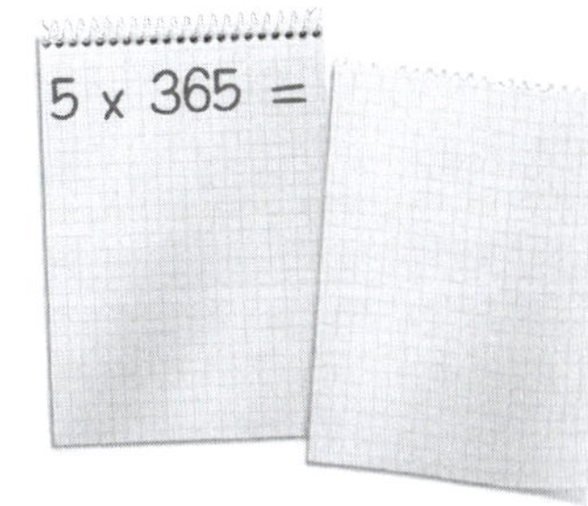

If Fiona starts today, then in a year she *will have made* **(make)** *1,825* pairs. She *will have spent* **(spend)** £ *1,825* on materials, but she *will have received* **(receive)** £ *9,125* from her customers. This means she *will have made* **(make)** a profit of £ *7,300*. Fiona needs £2,000 to pay for a trip to Africa, so she needs to sell *500* pairs. If she works twice as hard, she *will have earned* **(earn)** the money for her trip in only *50* days. And as a student, she *won't have had to* **(not have to)** pay any tax.

4 Some predictions about the future of work (PB p. 27/ex. 4)

a) Complete the sentences with the verbs below to say what will be happening or will have happened in the future. Put the verbs in the ***future perfect*** or ***future progressive.***

become **become** **do** **disappear** **lose**

make **replace** **run** **stay** **work**

1. An increasing number of people *will be working* from home in future.
2. Even schoolchildren *will be running* their own businesses from their bedrooms then.
3. In 20 years' time, laptops *will have replaced* desktop computers.
4. Fax machines *will have become* a thing of the past by the year 2050.
5. By the end of this century, women *will be doing* all the top management jobs.
6. At the same time, more men *will be staying* at home to look after the children.
7. Within the next 30 years, the more traditional agricultural jobs *will have disappeared*.
8. Instead, more people *will be making* a living from jobs in service industries.
9. By 2040 factories in developing countries *will have become* more productive.
10. However, by then a lot of unskilled factory workers *will have lost* their jobs because of new technological developments.

b) Give your own opinion about two of the predictions in **a)**. Say how likely you think they are, and whether they are a good thing. Give reasons for your opinions.

A personal statement

1 Looking at tenses (PB p. 28/ex. 1)

a) Read again Sandra Hickling's personal statement on page 28 of your book.
Then write down the questions. Be careful with the tenses.

b) Now answer the questions in your exercise book. Remember to write full sentences.
(Erwartungshorizont: S. 77)

1. how many • A level subjects • Sandra • study • at the moment?

   How many A level subjects is Sandra studying at the moment?

2. how • she • find • the subjects • so far?

   How has she found the subjects so far?

3. the course • cover • graphic design?

   Does the course cover graphic design?

4. she • think of doing • Graphic Design at university?

   Is she thinking of doing Graphic Design at university?

5. she • ever • do • a work placement?

   Has she ever done a work placement?

6. what • she • do • at SunSpot Electronics?

   What did she do at SunSpot Electronics?

7. she • design • the school homepage • by herself?

   Did she design the school homepage by herself?

8. what • the school website group • do • now?

   What is the school website group doing now?

9. why • Sandra • not be able to • use • the program • when • it • be • ready?

   Why won't Sandra be able to use the program when it's ready?

10. Sandra • compete • in a marathon • in April?

    Will Sandra be competing/Is she competing/going to compete in a marathon in April?

11. when • Sandra • join • her band?

    When did Sandra join her band?

12. they • have • any concerts • yet?

    Have they had any concerts yet?

13. Sandra • be • worried about going • to university?

    Is Sandra worried about going to university?

2 What about you? (PB p. 29/ex. 3)

a) Use these questions to interview your partner and make notes of the answers.

b) Use your notes to write a short report about your partner. Ask him/her to check it for any mistakes.

1. What are your favourite subjects at school? Would you like to study any of them at university?
2. Do you belong to any clubs at school? Why did you join, or not join them?
3. Have you ever been involved in charity events? What did you do?
4. What are your hobbies? Do you think they will be helpful in your future career? Why, or why not?
5. Do you enjoy travelling? Describe some interesting trips you have been on.

3 Letter from Australia (PB p. 29/ex. 4)

Put in the verbs on the right in the e-mail below. Use the ***simple present*** or ***present progressive***. One of the verbs is in the ***past progressive***.

belong to | cost | enjoy | have | have | hope | look | need | prefer | see | seem | smell | taste | think | think of

Hi, Steve,

Mum and I ___*are having*___ a great time here in Australia. We ___*are enjoying*___ every minute of it. My grandma ___*looks*___ a lot like my mum, but she's older, of course. Grandpa is great fun – he is 82 and even ___*belongs to*___ a surfing club! I've met lots of relatives already, and this afternoon we ___*are having*___ a barbie. Grandma is cooking the food and it ___*smells*___ fantastic. Mum burnt her lips while she ___*was tasting*___ one of grandma's special sauces – she ___*is seeing*___ the doctor at the moment. My Uncle Scott ___*is thinking of*___ moving to England. He ___*thinks*___ he'll have more opportunities in London, but I ___*prefer*___ the lifestyle here! Things ___*cost*___ less and everyone ___*seems*___ so friendly and relaxed, maybe because of the warm climate. Nobody ___*needs*___ to wear warm clothes and their favourite words are "No worries!". Anyway, I ___*hope*___ you're missing me as much as I missing you!

Love and kisses,
Sandra ❤❤❤❤❤

4 Future forms (PB p. 29/ex. 4) *(Erwartungshorizont: S. 77)*

List the different future forms you have learnt. For each one, write an example sentence in your exercise book and name the form.

Skills: Applying for a job

1 How to structure an application letter (PB p. 30/ex. 1)

The boxes show the structure of an application letter for an internship. Put in the right numbers for each part.

1 Yours sincerely,
2 Name and address of the person I am writing to.
3 More details about myself, referring to important points in my CV and my plans for the future.
4 My signature.
5 Introduction (how I heard about the organisation, who I am and why I am writing).
6 List of documents that I am enclosing.
7 What I would like to do during the internship and what I can bring to the organisation.
8 Heading to say what the letter is about.
9 My name (printed).
10 Dear Sir or Madam/Dear (+ name),
11 A polite and friendly ending that sums up the letter and expresses the hope for a reply.
12 Date on which the letter was written.
13 My address.

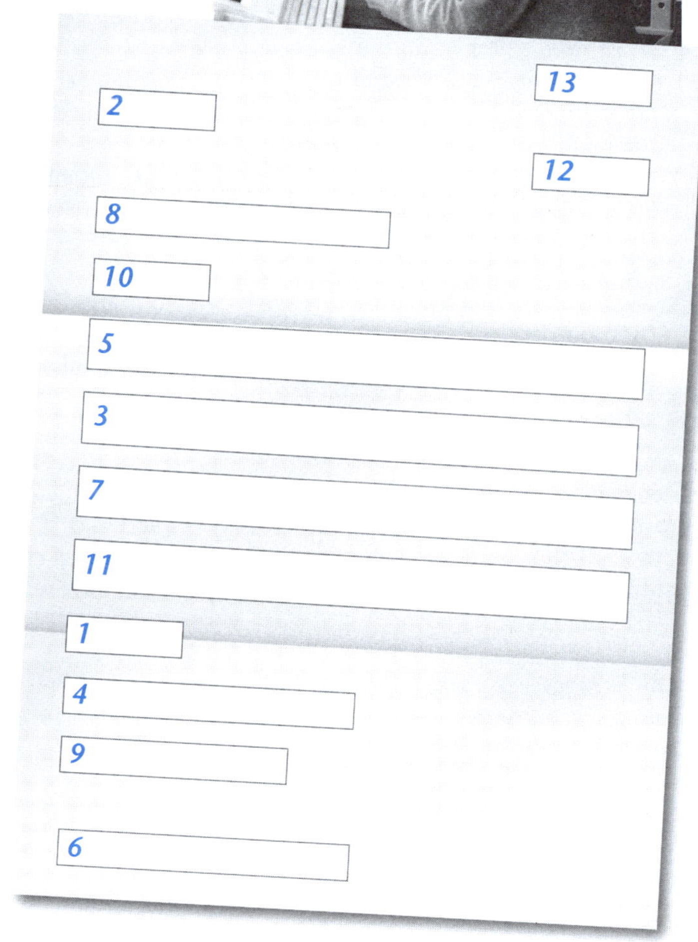

2 Phrase power (PB p. 30/ex. 1)

a) In which part of the letter would you expect to find these phrases? Put in the right numbers.

[3] I am enclosing my résumé, which shows …

[5] I would like an internship to improve my English and gain experience of working in the USA.

[11] I would be pleased to have the opportunity of an internship at the City Playhouse, and hope to hear from you soon.

[3] I have a good knowledge of English.

[5] I read about the City Playhouse on your homepage with great interest.

[3] As far as my studies are concerned, I will be taking my High School Diploma exams in two years. After that, I hope to go on to college to study Drama and Dance.

[7] I would be very interested in working behind the scenes at the City Playhouse, and I believe that I will be able to make a contribution to the success of your show.

[3] You will also see that I am a member of the local drama club.

b) Find similar phrases in Julia Lehmann's letter on page 30 of your book. Write them in your exercise book.

1 A recipe for success (PB p. 33/ex. 3)

Here is an interview with Penny and Joe, who founded a successful new business called Soupa-Soup.
Put in the missing questions above the answers.

- What is it like working for Soupa-Soup?
- Where did you get the idea for takeaway soups?
- So what's new at Soupa-Soup?
- What was the turning point?
- What problems did you have at first?
- What is your recipe for success?
- How does Soupa-Soup help the community?
- So how did your business start?

1. **How did the two of you meet?**
We were both friends at college, where we were studying Marketing. We often talked about starting our own business, but of course we had no money and no experience.

2. *Where did you get the idea for takeaway soups?*
We wanted an idea that would make money but also be good for people. Our cafeteria only sold fast food, mostly burgers and chips. One day we heard a student complaining that there wasn't any healthy food for vegetarians, so we came up with the idea of selling takeaway soups made from nothing but vegetables.

3. *So how did your business start?*
After college, we both got jobs in advertising, but two years later we were still talking about our idea, so we decided to act. We set up a stall at the Edinburgh Festival, bought some vegetables for £500 and spent the whole day making soup. We put up a sign which said "Do you think we should give up our jobs to make these soups?" with a YES box and a NO box. We asked customers to throw their empty soup mug in the box of their choice, and by the end of the day the YES box was full. The next day, we gave up our jobs.

4. *What problems did you have at first?*
Our business idea was a big risk. At first, we couldn't persuade anyone to invest in our idea. Some people said it wasn't possible to sell soup without additives. The worst moment was when the tenth bank manager laughed at the idea, but we never gave up.

5. *What was the turning point?*
With no money, we decided to give a presentation to a group of 'business angels' – people who invest money in start-ups. They all refused to give us money except for a wealthy Scottish businessman who lent us £30,000. Since then we have grown rapidly. Now we're making £20 million a year.

6. *What is it like working for Soupa-Soup?*
Super! There are over 90 people working for the company, which is based in Edinburgh. Everyone has their own laptop, so they can work anywhere they like in the building, or they can relax on big sofas in a room we call the 'Comfort Zone'. And of course there's a fantastic canteen called the 'Soupabowl' with free soup for staff and visitors to taste.

7. *How does Soupa-Soup help the community?*
We give 10 percent of our profits each year to support the countries where we buy our vegetables. We also raise money for charities to help old people. Last month we held a mug-painting competition. All sorts of customers took part, from top fashion designers to grandmas! We sold the mugs and raised £3,000 which we gave to charities.

8. *So what's new at Soupa-Soup?*
We have developed 25 different soup recipes and we're always looking for new ingredients and tastes. At the moment we only sell vegetarian soup, but we're thinking of introducing soups with meat or fish. It's a big decision, and we're not sure which way to go.

9. *What is your recipe for success?*
We think it's important that people eat healthily. Of course, you can't do that all the time – we ourselves enjoy chips now and then – but you need to get enough good stuff, too. To be successful in business, you need to believe in what you do and be honest with your customers.

2 What's wrong here? (PB p. 33/ex. 3)

There is a mistake in each of these sentences. Find and correct them. Work with a partner.

1. Joe and Penny dreamed of starting their own business while they were still ~~Law~~ students at college. *Marketing*
2. They developed their idea after a student complained there was ~~too much~~ food for vegetarians. *not enough/too little*
3. ~~Three~~ years later, they decided to try out their idea at the Edinburgh Festival. *Two*
4. Customers could put their empty soup ~~bowls~~ in a YES box or a NO box. *mugs*
5. The soup was so popular with the customers that Penny and Joe gave up their jobs in advertising ~~a few days later~~. *the next day*
6. It was hard to find people who would invest in their idea, but in the end they raised £30,000 from a ~~group of business angels~~. *(wealthy) Scottish businessman*
7. Now the company is highly successful, with ~~nearly~~ 90 members of staff. *over*
8. The 'Soupabowl' is a wonderful canteen where visitors and staff can ~~buy~~ soups. *try/taste*
9. Soupa-Soup give a tenth of their profits to countries ~~that buy~~ their vegetables. *where they buy*

3 Words for words (PB p. 33/ex. 3)

Find words in the text on page 22 that fit these definitions. Try to guess new words from the context.

1. people who refuse to eat meat: *vegetarians*
2. to encourage somebody (and cause them) to do something: *persuade*
3. things that are added to food to improve it or keep it fresh: *additives*
4. another word for 'rich': *wealthy*
5. to collect money for something: *raise*
6. the different foods used in cooking: *ingredients*
7. adjective to describe someone who tells the truth: *honest*

4 Creative writing: A businessman's advice (PB p. 33/ex. 3)

Penny and Joe have asked the Scottish businessman, Doug Tate, for advice on whether to sell soup with meat or fish. Write his reply in which he advises them and suggests a meeting to discuss details (160–180 words).

5 Role play: An interactive presentation (PB p. 33/ex. 3)

Choose one of these tasks and work either with a partner or in a group of four or five people.

A You are Penny and Joe. Give a presentation in which you 'sell' your idea to a group of business angels. Say how much money you need and why. Be prepared to answer difficult questions.

B You are a group of business angels. Prepare questions that you want to ask Penny and Joe about their business idea. Listen to their presentation and make notes. At the end, ask questions that will help you decide whether or not to invest in the project.

6 Mediation: Translating key information (PB p. 36/ex. 9)

Bavaria's Best

VERKÄUFER/INNEN GESUCHT FÜR OKTOBERFEST

Teilzeit, evtl. auch Vollzeit (25/40 Std. Woche)

- Laden für Originalprodukte aus Bayern sucht engagierte und kontaktfreudige Verkäufer/innen mit guten Englischkenntnissen, um unser dynamisches Verkaufsteam während des Oktoberfests zu unterstützen.
- Sie haben Erfahrung im Verkauf und können gut mit Kunden aus verschiedenen Ländern umgehen. Außerdem sind Sie freundlich, zuverlässig und belastbar sowie auch bereit, gelegentlich sonntags zu arbeiten. Bei uns finden Sie ein tolles Arbeitsklima mit der Möglichkeit einer Weiterbildung.
- Befristeter Vertrag (max. 6 Wochen)
- Lohn nach Vereinbarung + Leistungsbonus

Interessiert?
Dann bewerben Sie sich schriftlich mit Lebenslauf bis Ende Juli bei:

Bavaria's Best
Thomas Ketterer
Königstraße 2
80539 München

a) Read the advertisement. Then help Thomas Ketterer to advertise the job on the internet.
Put in the details in English. *(Erwartungshorizont)*

Name of company:	*Bavaria's Best*
Type of business and activity:	*shop that sells products from Bavaria/ original Bavarian products*
Position:	*shop/sales assistant(s)*
Duties:	*supporting/helping sales team during Oktoberfest*
Qualifications/ experience:	*sales experience*
Personal qualities required:	*good at dealing with customers from different countries; friendly, reliable and can work under pressure*
Duration of employment[1]:	*up to six weeks/six weeks or less*
Hours:	*25/40 hours per week; Sundays if necessary*
Pay and conditions:	*will be/can be discussed; extra money for good work*
How to apply:	*written application with Curriculum Vitae*
Contact details:	*Bavaria's Best, Thomas Ketterer, Königstraße 2, 80539 München*
Application deadline:	*end of July*

b) Would you like to do this job? Explain in a few sentences what you would like or not like about it. Write in your exercise book.

c) Write a letter of application in English for the job. Look again at page 21 to help you with the application.

[1] [djʊəˌreɪʃn‿əv‿ɪmˈplɔɪmənt] – Beschäftigungsdauer

1 Word power (PB p. 37/ ex. 1)

Across →

1. Adjective of 'compete'.
5. Thank you for your letter ☐ 5 July.
6. Lawyers help people to keep out of ☐.
8. The price of something.
10. Opposite of 'lose'.
11. To ☐ experience.
12. Stealing is against the ☐.
13. Person who is willing to work for nothing.
17. Something you have done that you are proud of.

Down ↓

1. BE for 'résumé' (two words).
2. You can make a loss or a ☐.
3. Candidates for a job.
4. AE for 'work placement'.
7. Your name as you write it by hand.
9. Opposite of 'bought'.
14. To ☐ a time and a place.
15. To ☐ up a new company.
16. To continue = to carry ☐.

2 Typical mistakes (PB p. 37/ ex. 3) *(Lösung: S. 77)*

Underline the mistakes and write the correct sentences in your exercise book.

Example: I would like having my own company. **(verb form)**
I would like to have my own company.

1. We want to rise money for old people. **(word)**
2. I'm really looking forward to start college. **(verb form)**
3. I'm a member of a band since seven months. **(tense, word)**
4. I think of doing a work placement by the tax office. **(tense, preposition)**
5. My mother is lawyer. **(article)**
6. Can you borrow me £200! **(word, punctuation)**
7. This cream is for sensible skin. **(false friend)**
8. We're leaving early tomorrow so we need to get up until 4 am. **(preposition)**
9. This ice cream is tasting deliciously! **(tense, word form)**
10. I would like to make things, that I can sell. **(punctuation)**
11. Three years ago I have taken part in a exchange programme. **(tense, article)**
12. I speak fluently English. **(word order or word form)**
13. I'm afraid but I can't come today. I come tomorrow. **(word not necessary, tense)**
14. This time tomorrow I will lie on the beach! **(tense)**

General revision

1 Teenagers in the US want more family time

(PB p. 38/ex. 1)

Complete the sentences with ***gerunds*** or ***infinitives***. Sometimes you will need to use a preposition.

As kids grow up, it's quite natural for them *to want* (**want**) *to hang out* (**hang out**) more with their friends instead *of being* (**be**) with their parents all the time. However, a recent US survey shows that many young people would actually like *to spend* (**spend**) more time with their parents, but say their parents seem *to be* (**be**) too busy. *Having* (**have**) regular family mealtimes has a positive effect, and teenagers who are used *to eating* (**eat**) dinner with a parent five days a week or more are less likely *to smoke* (**smoke**) or *(to) drink* (**drink**) alcohol, and fewer of these teenagers try *taking* (**take**) drugs[1]. Although they know it's important for their kids *to have* (**have**) all the 'stuff' they need, many parents apparently don't stop *to think* (**think**) that *spending* (**spend**) time with their teenage children and *listening* (**listen**) to their views is just as important.

[1][drʌgz] – Drogen

2 Different situations – different forms (PB p. 38/ex. 2)

a) Which ***future form*** fits the situation best?

I'll have taken • I'm taking • I'll take • I'm going to take • I'll be taking

1. "Oh, Mum, look at the time! I'm going to be late for school!" – "It's OK, *I'll take* you in the car. I have to deal with something in town anyway."
2. "I'm so looking forward to the end of June! By that time, *I'll have taken* all my exams!"
3. "Have you made any arrangements for next year yet?" – "Yes, *I'm taking* a year off to travel the world. Starting in September, probably!"
4. "Think of me next year at this time! I'll be in Australia by then. *I'll be taking* photos of kangaroos in the outback!"
5. "I'm much too hot in this jacket! *I'm going to take* it off!"

b) In all these sentences the wrong verb forms have been used. Decide which ***future forms*** would be more suitable. Write in your exercise book. Then compare your answers with a partner's. *(Lösung: S. 77)*

1. "Come on! We miss the beginning of the film if we won't hurry. It's starting at 8.30."
2. "Think of me tomorrow at this time. I'll take my driving test."
3. "I'll buy Sam a DVD for his birthday." – "Good idea. I help you to choose one."
4. "By next autumn I've left school. With a bit of luck I've started university."

3 What's that in English? (PB p. 39/ex. 3) *(Erwartungshorizont)*

When people are talking to you in English, it's quite natural for ideas to come into your head in German sometimes! How would you put these ideas into English?

What are you looking for? — Meine Brille! Hast du sie irgendwo gesehen?

Where did you get your fantastic black jeans? — Ich habe sie in München gekauft. Gefällt sie dir?

1. *My glasses! Have you seen them anywhere?*
2. *I bought them in Munich. Do you like them?*

What sort of job do you think you'd most like to do when you leave school? — Ich möchte Fotograf werden. Das wäre bestimmt ein ganz interessanter Beruf.

Was there anything on the news about that girl that was kidnapped yesterday? — Die Nachrichten im Radio waren sehr kurz. Die Polizei hat bisher keine Informationen erhalten.

3. *I'd like to be a photographer. I'm sure that would be quite an interesting job.*
4. *The news on the radio was very short. The police haven't got/received any information so far.*

4 Mixed bag: The three-year-old boy and his car (PB p. 39/ex. 4)

Complete the text with the missing words. Be careful with any verb forms.

John and Rachel Neal couldn't believe it *when* they received a message *from* eBay one evening *about* a car they *had* bought. "We *had* no idea what *was* happening," said Rachel. "*Neither* of us had *bought* anything! But when *we* checked, we discovered it *was* a pink Japanese car *that* we'd bought for £8,999. *Naturally*, we were both in a panic!"

The next *morning/day*, when their three-year-old *son* Jack woke *up*, he *told* his parents: "I've *bought* a car!" Rachel said: "I must *have* left my eBay password in my computer. Jack's brilliant on the PC, *although* he's only three. He *was* watching me when I last *bid* for something *on* eBay, so he *knew* how to do it!" John called Paul Jones, the seller *of* the car, and *explained* the mistake. *Luckily*, he saw the funny side and said he *would* advertise the car again. "As soon *as* I heard it was a *little* boy who *had* done it *by* mistake, I cancelled the bid," said Mr Jones. "It was *no* problem!"

From: The Guardian (adapted)

5 Listening: Cell phones in schools? (PB p. 41/ex. 7)

a) Listen to this TV programme. Then read the sentences on the right before you listen again. Tick ✔ the correct statements. Sometimes more than one answer may be right.

b) Write an e-mail (50–100 words) to the TV programme and give your own opinion on this topic. Use your exercise book.
(Erwartungshorziont: S. 77)

1. Taking cell phones to school is illegal
- ☐ a) in most US states.
- ☐ b) everywhere in the US.
- ✔ c) in over twenty US states.

2. Tom Bailey has had trouble with
- ☐ a) a student who brought a pizza to school.
- ✔ b) cell phones that ring in class.
- ✔ c) students that send text messages.

3. At Helen's school in New York City,
- ✔ a) most students bring their cell phones.
- ☐ b) cell phones are allowed.
- ✔ c) there has been trouble with films on students' phones.

4. Jane Blomberg thinks
- ☐ a) it's unnecessary for kids to have cell phones.
- ✔ b) life in big cities is dangerous.
- ✔ c) kids should be able to contact their parents.

6 Reading comprehension: Should girls play football with the boys? (PB p. 41/ex. 7)

It has become another front in the battle of the sexes, fought in playgrounds and sports clubs across the country: Should girls be allowed to play football with the boys at school? Today, an influential committee of MPs[1] says that they should, and demands that the Football Association (FA) change its rules so mixed teams are allowed beyond the age of 11.

Women's football soared in popularity after the huge success of the film 'Bend It Like Beckham', overtaking netball as the biggest female participation sport. It has 130,000 registered players and expanded from 80 teams affiliated to the FA in 1993 to more than 8,000 last season.

But, according to the MPs' report, it receives too little support from the men's Premiership clubs. The report also notes there are no women on the FA's board.

The MPs admit that progress has been made, thanks to live BBC coverage of the 2005 European women's championship, which attracted 3 million viewers for England's matches, and that attitudes have changed since the FA declared in 1921 that the game was "unsuitable for females".

MPs' support for mixed teams above the age of 11 follows a campaign led by 10-year-old Minnie Cruttwell, who wrote to Tessa Jowell, the culture secretary, asking to be allowed to continue to play for her south London team next season. "The rule is sexist," she explained. "It's not fair that I have to change teams, because I'm just as good as boys." The MPs agree that selection should be on ability, but weight and height should also be considered.

The committee chairman said: "The FA has done a lot for women but it can do more." It should take a lead in removing cultural and practical barriers that undermine the women's game. The report criticises clubs such as Manchester United for withdrawing support from their women's teams, and wants men's professional clubs to share their training grounds with women's clubs.

Helen Donohoe, head of the Women's Sports Foundation, said: "One in three girls wants to play football." But often they simply don't get enough encouragement.

From: The Guardian (adapted)

[1]MP = Member of Parliament

a) Fill in the gaps to show you have understood the text.

Members of *Parliament* want the British Football Association to let girls over *eleven* play in school *teams* with *boys*. In recent years, women's football has become much more *popular*, but men's clubs still *don't* give women enough *support*. A campaign started when a *girl* of ten didn't want to *have* to play for a different *team* after her eleventh birthday. The MPs agree that teams should be *chosen* according to how *well* people play, and whether they are *tall* or heavy enough. Their report demands that *men's* clubs should allow *women* to *play/practise* on their grounds. At least 30 *percent* of all girls would *like* to play football, but often they aren't *encouraged* to do so.

b) Find phrases in the text that have a similar meaning.

1. disagreement between men and women: *battle of the sexes (line 1)*
2. not good for women: *unsuitable for females (line 25)*
3. boys and girls playing together: *mixed teams (line 27)*

c) React to this statement, and give reasons for your opinion for or against. Write about 100 words in your exercise book.

Letting girls play football in the same team as boys **is crazy!**

7 A pocket money survey (PB p. 41/ex. 7)

The twelve words in the box are missing from this text – but they are not in the right order. Find the right place for each word and write it in. Use each word only once.

a • as • between • both • feared • goes • ~~how~~ • of • percent • software • to • whereas

A survey of *how* children spend their pocket money shows what most parents have always *feared*: more than half of the average child's weekly money *goes* on sweets, snacks, games and films. Only about 7 *percent* is spent on books and magazines. Not surprisingly, the survey found that girls spend six times *as* much as boys on 'personal care' products such as deodorants. By the age *of* thirteen, girls have already started *to* spend almost twice as much as boys on clothes and shoes. An average of 20 percent *a* week of boys' money is spent on games, hobbies and pets, *whereas* girls spend less in these areas. But the difference *between* boys and girls is greatest when it comes to computer *software* and games, for which boys spend eleven times as much as girls. Mobile phones are used by *both* sexes equally.

From: The Independent (adapted)

Relationships

1 Are you a mate in a million? (PB p. 42/ex. 1)

If you want to be a really good mate, make sure you don't ever do any of these things …

A You leave your mate out of things:
Feeling left out is awful. Maybe everyone's discussing who'll be sharing rooms on the school trip but nobody's asked you yet. You feel sick – what if you're left on your own?

B You're jealous of your mate:
If your mate looks brilliant, has got cool clothes and is popular with everybody – it's natural to feel a bit jealous! But there are ways you can deal with this.

C When you borrow your mate's things, you 'forget' to give them back:
OK, sometimes your mate seems to have nicer clothes – or just the CD you want to borrow. But it's not fair to keep things too long.

D You're copying your mate:
If you like your mate's clothes or hairstyle, it's natural to want to copy them. But being copied – especially by your mate – can be SO annoying!

E You talk about your mate behind their back:
Being a great mate means standing up for your friend if you hear anyone saying unkind things about them.

F You want your mate all to yourself:
You've been best mates for ages. Now you notice your friend wants to have other friends, too. You try to prevent this – a BIG mistake!

From: SHOUT Magazine

a) Now read the pieces of advice below and match them with the points above. Write the letters **A** to **F** in the correct boxes.

b) Add an extra piece of advice (your own!) to each section. *(Erwartungshorizont)*

C Never keep anything you've been lent for longer than a few days.	**F** It's good to be friendly with lots of people. Don't think others may 'steal' your mate.	**B** Why not just be honest? Say "You're so lucky" and laugh about it with your mate.
Look after things you've been lent, so they still look fine when you return them.	*Try to see other people as possible friends for you both!*	*Remember that you've got a lot of good points, too!*
D Remember: what's right for your mate may not suit YOU!	**E** Imagine how you'd feel if they were talking about you!	**A** Try to treat your mate the way YOU'd like to be treated.
Perhaps your mate can advise you about what suits you best.	*Always stand up for a friend when others are saying nasty things.*	*Make sure your mate knows what's going on and include her/him.*

⟨c)⟩ Behaving really badly can sometimes mean the end of a friendship. Think of an example and describe in a few sentences how this might happen. Write in your exercise book.

2 What friendship means (PB p. 43/ex. 3) *(Erwartungshorizont: S. 77)*

Think of an everyday situation to fit each of these characteristics. Write in your exercise book.
Example: **helpful:** Sarah is having trouble with her homework, so she rings her friend Kate. Kate explains how to do it over the phone – or goes to Sarah's house. She's a really helpful person!

A good friend is … helpful | tactful | sympathetic | reliable | honest | fun to be with

1 Bad habits (PB p. 45/ex. 2) *(Erwartungshorizont: S. 77)*

Read what John says about himself, his family and one of his teachers – and their 'bad habits'!
What else might he say? Add extra sentences with ***always***. Write in your exercise book.
Start like this: 1. I'm always buying things like hamburgers and …

1. I eat far too much fast food.
2. My brother can be a bit of a show-off.
3. My little sister is crazy about fashion.
4. My parents worry too much about my future.
5. But it's true – I don't do enough work for school.
6. Our Maths teacher seems to think his subject is more important than anything else!

2 Wrong again! (PB p. 45/ex. 2) *(Erwartungshorizont)*

Correct these statements with the help of the information in brackets. Use ***It was … who/that …***
Example: The Backstreet Boys were the first big American boy band. **(New Kids On The Block)**
➜ That's not true! It was New Kids On The Block who were the first big American boy band.

1. Britney Spears made a great album called 'Back to Basics'. **(Christina Aguilera)**

   Wrong! *It was Christina Aguilera who made an album called 'Back to Basics'.*

2. Grunge started in San Francisco. **(Seattle)**

   That's not true! It was in Seattle that Grunge started.

3. The Bloodhound Gang had a big hit with 'Dani California'. **(Red Hot Chili Peppers)**

   No, it was the Red Hot Chili Peppers who had a big hit with 'Dani California'.

4. The Spice Girls announced their break-up in 2005. **(2001)**

   Wrong! It was in 2001 that they announced their break-up.

5. Madonna and her husband adopted a child from South America. **(a child from Africa)**

   That's not true! It was a child from Africa that they adopted.

6. Louis Armstrong? Oh yes, he was the first man on the moon. **(Neil Armstrong)**

   No, it was Neil Armstrong who was the first man on the moon.

3 Is it the same with you? (PB p. 45/ex. 3)

a) Talk about the statements below with a partner. Think about how you can reply to them.

b) Write your answers in your exercise book. *(Erwartungshorizont: S. 77)*
Example: "My parents never let me have big parties." – "Neither do mine. They're so strict!/ But mine do. They don't mind how many people I invite!"

1. "I've got a TV in my room at home."
2. "My parents both work full-time."
3. "My mother can't help me at all with my French homework."
4. "We sometimes have fish on Fridays."
5. "I'd hate to be a teacher!"
6. "We never go to exciting places on holiday."
7. "My father sometimes takes me to school in the car."
8. "I never seem to have enough pocket money!"

4 What would you say? (PB p. 45/ex. 4) *(Erwartungshorizont)*

What might you say in these situations? Use the words in brackets and the pictures on the right to add emphasis.

1. Your friend has got a really great new hairstyle. **(do)**

   I *do like your new hairstyle!*

2. Every time you buy something new to wear, your mate decides to get the same thing! **(always)**

   You're *always buying the same things as I've got!*

3. You've just found out that your friend Daisy fancies your brother (NOT the boy you thought!). **(it's)**

   So *it's my brother (that) Daisy fancies!*

4. You are feeling wet and cold after a long walk home in the rain. **(what)**

   What I need is a nice hot bath!

5. Your friend can't come to stay over the weekend and you are very disappointed about that. **(terribly)**

   I'm terribly sorry you can't come next weekend!

5 Error spotting: An embarrassing moment (PB p. 45/ex. 4)

Anja wants to mail her English friend Melissa. Are the underlined words and phrases correct or not? Use the lines to correct the words where necessary. If there is no mistake, write the word 'correct'.

I must tell you from (1) something really awful that has happened (2) to me last Saturday! I was on a party (3) at a friend's house. While I was dancing, I saw suddenly (4) this fantastic lad that I've fancied for absolutely ages! I was wearing this fab new jeans (5) and a really COOL top, and my confidence was pretty high (6), so I decided to go up to him to introduce me (7). When I was just a few feet away from him, I slipped and fell (8). The next moment I was laying (9) on the floor in front of him. When I was looking up (10), he and his mates were all laughing at me. It was terrible! I can say you (11), I've never felt so embarassed (12) in all my life!

1. *about*
2. *happened*
3. *at a party*
4. *suddenly saw*
5. *these fab new jeans*
6. *correct*
7. *introduce myself*
8. *correct*
9. *was lying*
10. *looked up*
11. *can tell you*
12. *embarrassed*

1 George and his parents (PB p. 47/ex. 2) *(Erwartungshorizont: S. 78)*

a) Some time before his first big party, George filled in this questionnaire in a teen magazine. Use ***let*** and ***make*** to explain what his parents were like then. Write in your exercise book.
You can start: 1. They let him …

How liberal-minded are your parents?	Yes	No
Are you allowed to have parties at home?	✗	
Do you have to tidy your room regularly?		✗
Are you expected to do jobs in the house or garden?		✗
Are you allowed to smoke in the house?		✗
Can you watch TV as long as you like?	✗	
Do they expect you to say where you're going and when you'll be back?	✗	
Can you camp and spend weekends away with friends?	✗	

b) What do you think life will be like for George after the party? Write in your exercise book.
You can start: They certainly won't let him have … They probably …

2 Everyday English: Useful phrases with *let* and *make* (PB p. 47/ex. 2) *(Erwartungshorizont: S. 78)*

Complete these dialogues. Use the phrases in the box and add your own ideas to finish each sentence. Write in your exercise book.

Let them think • It makes you wonder • Don't let it worry you • I'll let you know • That made me realize • It made me laugh

1. "I can easily meet you at the station." – "Great! …"
2. "Judy was really sympathetic when Mark broke it off with you, wasn't she?" – "Yeah. …"
3. "That was one of the most amusing films I've ever seen!" – "You're right. …"
4. "Polly's got another new pair of designer jeans!" – "I know. …"
5. "Sue's always saying nasty things about me behind my back." – "Well! …"
6. "Everybody says you were mean to dump Joe!" – "I don't care! …"

3 Having it done (PB p. 47/ex. 3)

What do these people say? Use ***have something done*** and choose from the verbs on the right. (Be careful with the tenses!)

deliver **wash** **clean** **cut** **make** **repair**

1. *Mum:* Your hair's so long, George! Please go into town and *have it cut*.
2. *George:* We needn't get all those heavy drinks for the party at the supermarket, need we?
   We *can have them delivered* by 'Partyline', can't we?
3. *Tim:* Look, my watch is working OK again! I *'ve had it repaired*!
4. *Mark:* Can you wash my curtains, Mum? Or should we *have them cleaned*?
5. *Sue:* Surely there's something we can do with all the little apples on that tree!
   What about *having them made* into cider?
6. *Dad:* The car looks a lot better, doesn't it? I *had it washed* yesterday.

4 English expressions for the German verb 'lassen' (PB p. 47/ex. 4)

Complete the dialogues with suitable forms of ***let/make* + *object* + *infinitive*** or ***have something done.***

1. "Why wasn't Kim at school today?" – "She *had* two teeth *pulled out* **(pull out)** yesterday afternoon. That *(has) made* her *feel* **(feel)** pretty awful."
2. "John's so lucky! His parents often *let* him *drive* **(drive)** their car." – "I know. When I learn to drive, I don't expect my parents *will let* me *use* **(use)** theirs!"
3. "My hair's such a mess!" – "What about *letting* it *grow* **(grow)** a bit? If you did that, I'm sure it *would make* you *look* **(look)** really nice."
4. "Have you mended that lamp, Dad?" – "I've tried, but I can't *make* it *work* **(work)**, I'm afraid. I think we'll have to *have* it *repaired* **(repair)**. I'll take it to Fuller's tomorrow and *let* them *deal* **(deal)** with it for us."
5. "Joanne looks somehow different!" – "Yeah, it's her nose. She *has had* it *made* **(make)** straighter. It *makes* her face *seem* **(seem)** softer, doesn't it?" – "Maybe you're right. But I must say, I'd never *let* anyone *change* **(change)** the shape of *my* nose!"

5 Word building: Liberal-minded (PB p. 47/ex. 4)

a) A lot of adjectives that describe people are made up of ***an adjective*** + ***a part of the body*** (or related words) + ***ed***, for example 'liberal-minded'. Use compounds that are made from some of the words in the boxes to describe these people. (Check the words in your dictionary.)

left • long • red • dark • narrow • short • big • heavy	+	mind • skin • hand • hair • sight • head • heart

1. Mike thinks he knows everything. He's terribly *big-headed*.
2. Sue never needs to use sunscreen. She's very *dark-skinned*.
3. Mum has to wear glasses for driving. She's a bit *short-sighted*.
4. Grandpa can't accept any opinions that are different from his own. He's so *narrow-minded*.
5. Dad's broken his right arm, but he can still write OK because he's *left-handed*.

b) Look up all the adjectives in the box on the left in your dictionary. How many other compounds like these can you find? Write at least three more sentences with them in your exercise book.
(Erwartungshorizont: S. 78)

1 Hard times for Hayley (PB p. 48/ex. 1)

Under pressure

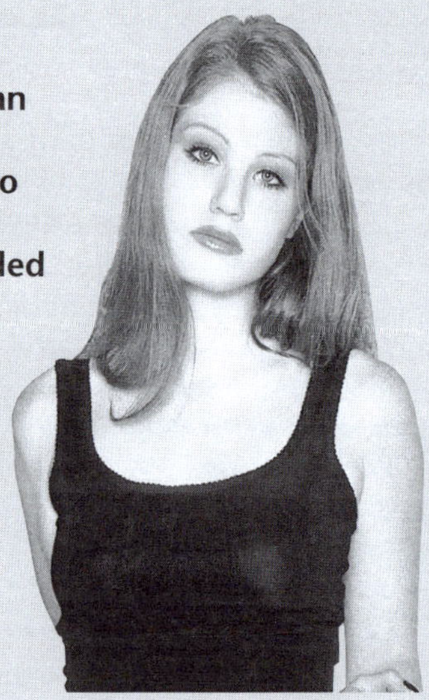

Hayley, 15, feels like an outcast because her parents can't afford to buy her fashionable clothes. She even ended up stealing from her mum to help make herself look trendy …

My mum and dad just don't have the money to buy me nice clothes. It's not because they're deliberately trying to make me look stupid or anything. Dad's on the dole and Mum only has a part-time job, so it's hard for them to pay the bills, never mind provide me with fashionable clothes. That doesn't make it any easier for me to take, though.

I know it's not Mum and Dad's fault, but they don't understand what I have to put up with. Our school is like a fashion show – although we're supposed to wear uniform, everyone still wears really fashionable stuff and loads of girls have got expensive jackets and shoes. I've got to make do with what my older sister has grown out of and it's obvious the stuff I'm wearing is really old and worn.

I've always felt as if everyone was talking about me but Mum just said I was imagining it. But she was wrong – this group of really fashionable girls started being mean to me, pulling at my clothes and telling me what a sad person I am because I don't have the right clothes.

Once they started, everyone else started picking on me, too, and it was really hard to take. My best mate, Mandy, said I should ignore them, but I just didn't find it that easy. I became so miserable that three times I just couldn't resist taking money out of Mum's purse. I was intending to buy something nice to wear but I realized I just couldn't. I felt so bad about doing it. After all, we were really short of money and anyway, how could I explain the new clothes to Mum and Dad? Mum did notice the money had gone missing, but she never once suspected me and that made me feel worse – she said to me that she knew my brother and I would never steal from her. I felt awful.

I still get teased at school about what I wear, but I just have to try and ignore it. It's hard, though, and I can't help getting upset. I just wish I could get the same clothes as everyone else. Then I'd be happy and those girls couldn't pick on me.

From: SHOUT Magazine

a) Explain the **marked** phrases in different words. Use an English-English dictionary to help you. Write in your exercise book. *(Erwartungshorizont: S. 78)*

1. line 1: Hayley, 15, **feels like an outcast**
2. line 3: her parents **can't afford to** buy her
3. line 15: Dad's **on the dole**
4. line 24: **loads of girls**
5. line 27: the stuff I'm wearing **is … worn**
6. line 39: I **was intending to buy** something
7. line 44: She **never once suspected me**
8. line 50: **can't help getting upset**

b) Use your dictionary, then underline the meaning that fits the context here.

1. **never mind** (line 17): it doesn't matter/don't worry/<u>and even more impossible</u>
2. **to make do with (s.th.)** (line 25): to wear/<u>to accept (although you don't like it)</u>/to deal with
3. **sad** (line 32): <u>boring and unfashionable</u>/unhappy/not so nice
4. **picking on (s.o.)** (line 34): choosing from a group/<u>treating unkindly and unfairly</u>/noticing

c) Find words from the text that would fit the context in these sentences. (Check your dictionary first!)

1. "Did Dave step on your shoes on purpose?" – "Yes, he did it ___*deliberately*___!"
2. "Where's that chocolate I bought?" – "I'm afraid it's all gone. I love chocolate and just couldn't ___*resist*___ eating it!"
3. "Is it true that Sally's run away?" – "I think so. She went ___*missing*___ about ten days ago."

A Reader's True Story

My sister is a runaway

Nine months ago my sixteen-year-old sister, Lesley, ran away from home. She told Mum she was going to school, but now we know she came home when the house was empty, packed some clothes, stole Mum's cash card and caught a bus to Glasgow.

When Mum and Dad first realized she'd gone, they thought she'd be back in a couple of hours. She often had arguments with Mum and Dad, but nothing too serious and she hadn't seemed too unhappy.

Lesley still hadn't come home a couple of days later, though, and when Mum and Dad found out that she'd taken the cash card and emptied Mum's bank account from machines round Glasgow, they knew it was serious.

Anyone who's thinking of running away from home should think about what it does to the rest of the family. I'd never seen my dad cry before, but he missed Lesley so much and was scared it was his fault she'd gone. He and Mum keep wondering if they should have been harder on her, or softer on her. They blame themselves for not realizing she was unhappy.

Her friends at school acted as if Lesley was some kind of star, as if she'd done something really brave and exciting instead of just selfish and stupid which is what I think.

Mum and Dad have spent nearly all their money on going to Glasgow looking for Lesley and paying for posters and leaflets to hand out asking if anyone's seen her. Mum's been to every drug and youth advice centre, although she knows they probably aren't allowed to say whether they've seen Lesley.

The only present Anna and her parents want this Christmas is for Anna's sister, Lesley, to come home …

Every weekend she and Dad still walk round the town centre late at night in case she's sleeping in a doorway, and they even go to concerts, looking for Lesley in the crowd. They come home tired and in tears because they haven't found her. It makes me feel almost guilty for being the one who's still here.

Mum used to look and act really young but now she's got a lot of grey hairs and takes tablets for depression. I hate Lesley for doing that to her.

Thanks to her, living with Mum and Dad can be hard. If the TV's on and something comes on about young girls being prostitutes or taking drugs I have to jump up and switch it off quickly, or Mum just starts to cry. Every time the phone rings I see Mum and Dad praying it might be Lesley – it never is, though.

Because of her I can't go out the door without Mum and Dad wanting to know every detail about where I'm going and if I'm ten minutes late from school Mum has almost called the police. Lesley did the stupid thing, but I'm the one who's paying for it.

It's nearly Christmas now – our first Christmas without her. I'm not looking forward to Christmas Day because I know how upset Mum and Dad are going to be. Even presents don't interest me. The only present I want is for Lesley to walk through the front door so we can be a proper family again. If you're reading this, Lesley – or if anyone who knows her is, can you tell her – please, please come home!

From: SHOUT Magazine

1 Understanding the text (PB p. 52/ex. 2) *(Erwartungshorizont: S. 78)*

a) Skim through the text quickly and sum up what you think it is about.

b) Now read the text carefully and underline any key words or information that seem important.

c) Answer the questions. Scan the text to find the information you need. The underlined words and phrases may help. Write in your exercise book.

1. Did Lesley have a good relationship with her parents?
2. When did they first realize the situation was serious?
3. How do they feel, now that their daughter has gone?
4. How have they tried to find Lesley?
5. How has life changed at home for Anna after what her sister has done?

2 Different reactions (PB p. 52/ex. 2) *(Erwartungshorizont: S. 78)*

a) Write down words and phrases from the text that describe how different people react to Lesley's disappearance. Make a grid in your exercise book.

Mum	Dad	Both parents	Anna	School friends

b) Then work with a partner to discuss what you think about these reactions. Why do you think they are so different? Whose feelings do you understand best?

3 Creative writing: A letter from Lesley (PB p. 52/ex. 2) *(Erwartungshorizont: S. 78)*

a) Sum up in a few sentences what we find out about Lesley from the text. Use your exercise book.

b) The text does not actually tell us very much about Lesley. First think of five questions that the text does not answer. Then imagine possible answers. Work in small groups.
Example: Why did Lesley decide to leave home?

c) A few weeks later, Lesley writes a letter to say how she is now, and to explain what made her leave home. Decide who you think she might write to (a school friend/a relative/…) and write the letter for her.

10 4 Listening: Wish you weren't here! (PB p. 52/ex. 2)

a) Listen to part of another 'Mates and Dates' programme. Then complete the sentences to show that you have understood the programme. Listen again if you need to. *(Erwartungshorizont)*

1. Younger kids usually *love/like* going on holiday with their parents, but teenagers feel *different about it*.
2. When Jody was in Italy with her parents, they wanted her to *be/arrive back by ten*.
3. Fourteen percent of all 15-year-olds *hate going on holiday with their parents*.
4. Holidays, like Christmas, count as *one of the most difficult times of the year*.

b) Now look at the questions below. Before you answer them in your exercise book, listen again. *(Erwartungshorizont: S. 78)*

1. What basic problem do young people often have when they go on holiday with their parents?
2. What was Jody's last holiday with her parents like?
3. In what way is 14 or 15 a 'difficult' age for holidays with parents?
4. What does Nick Fisher advise parents to do so that holidays will be more of a success?

c) What is your opinion on this subject? Talk in a small group about the problems you have experienced (or can imagine) and discuss possible solutions.

5 Mediation: Runaways in Germany (PB p. 53/ex. 3) *(Erwartungshorizont: S. 78)*

Scan the text below and mark the most important information in colour. Then put the main ideas into English. Keep the language as simple as you can. Write in your exercise book.

450 Kinder gelten in Deutschland als vermisst

Die meisten Ausreißer tauchen innerhalb einer Woche wieder auf

WIESBADEN – Die Hälfte aller Vermissten in Deutschland sind Kinder und Jugendliche. „Die meisten Fälle klären sich allerdings innerhalb der ersten Woche auf", sagte ein Sprecher des Bundeskriminalamtes (BKA) in Wiesbaden zum gestrigen „Tag des vermissten Kindes". „Nur drei Prozent bleiben länger als ein Jahr verschwunden." Am 31. März 2006 registrierte das BKA bundesweit rund 450 vermisste Kinder bis 13 Jahre. Hinzu kommen knapp 1200 Jugendliche zwischen 14 und 18 Jahren.

Eltern können nach Ansicht der Kriminalpolizei durch Aufmerksamkeit dazu beitragen, dass Kinder nicht aus Verzweiflung von zu Hause ausreißen. „Wenn die schulischen Leistungen nachlassen, die Kinder sich zurückziehen oder irgendwelche Probleme zu haben scheinen, sollten die Erwachsenen eine feine Antenne haben und mit den Kindern reden", sagte ein Sprecher des Landeskriminalamtes Niedersachsen, Detlef Ehrike. Viele Kinder laufen weg, wenn sie mit ihrem häuslichen und sozialen Umfeld unzufrieden sind und gleichzeitig einen neuen Freund kennen lernen, der sie in dieser Unzufriedenheit bestärkt. „Dies gilt vor allem für die erste Liebe in der Pubertät. Wenn die Tochter zum Beispiel das Gefühl hat, dass ihr erster Freund nicht von den Eltern akzeptiert wird, hält sie womöglich das Weglaufen für die beste Lösung", sagte Ehrike. (dpa)

6 Mediation: Letter to an agony aunt (PB p. 65/ex. 4) *(Erwartungshorizont: S. 78)*

What is Craig's problem and what is Eve's advice to him? Summarise them in German.

Dear Eve,

I'm so fed up with my parents. They're always ganging up against me. I'm 16 and I don't want to be told when to do my homework, go to bed, practise the piano, etc. I reckon I can decide for myself. OK, I admit that I hardly ever touch the piano. But all their moaning about the cost of the lessons isn't going to motivate me! They say if I don't pull my socks up at school I'll mess up my exams and end up among the unemployed, etc. Don't they understand that the more they go on, the less I listen? I just kind of switch off – a perfectly normal reaction as far as I'm concerned. They say I'm uncommunicative. Well, I can communicate with my friends OK. Mostly online, of course. But the time spent at my computer is another thing they can't handle. They say I'm frittering my life away, when everybody of my generation is doing the same. They just don't get it. Every day I have words like "spoilt", "ungrateful" and "lazy" thrown at me. I want to have a decent relationship with my folks, but they're making it hard for me. What can I do?

Craig, Swindon

Eve's reply

The teenage years can be a very turbulent time for you teenagers and your parents. You have to cope with many things: surging hormones and changing bodies, the need to find yourselves and re-align your social relationships, exam pressures. You can become prone to extreme mood swings. New research suggests that this erratic behaviour is partly due to the reorganisation that takes place in the brain at this age. Your parents, forgetting what this process was like, become over-protective. Disappointed that their child's enthusiasm and love of life has turned into monosyllabic grumpiness, they put this down to their failure as parents and try to be stricter, which leads to more conflict. Both sides need to relax. Your parents have your best interests at heart, so why not humour them by being more open? Talk about your feelings. Keep them informed about your online social relationships. Your letter suggests that you could exert yourself a bit more, so why not make a special effort? I'm sure you will find an improvement in the relationship with your parents.

1 Idioms with parts of the body (PB p. 54/ex. 1) *(Erwartungshorizont: S. 78)*

a) Use your English-English dictionary to complete these sentences. Then take your exercise book and explain the meaning of each idiom.

b) Write sentences in your exercise book with idioms that can be made with the words you didn't use in **a)**. Use your dictionary.

1. "We had been having arguments for days, and last night everything came to a *head*."
2. "I asked Sue if she wanted to join the band, but she turned her *nose* up at the idea."
3. "Can you give me a *hand* with the washing up?"
4. "I stayed out till 2 am last Saturday, and now Dad says he's going to put his *foot* down."
5. "Let's pay the bill. Can you try to catch the waiter's *eye*?"
6. "When I asked her to feed the pigs, she made a *face*."

2 *Let, make* or *have?* (PB p. 55/ex. 3) *(Erwartungshorizont: S. 78)*

help deliver plant laugh get understand

Finish what these people say in the way you think best. Use the verbs on the right with ***let, make*** or ***have***. Write in your exercise book.

1. My parents have no idea of my feelings. I just can't …
2. Don't you understand that maths problem? OK, …
3. You'll never believe how much I had to do in the garden last week! Dad …
4. I'm not going to try to cook for sixty people! I think …
5. We all thought that comedy on TV last night was very disappointing. It didn't …
6. Have the soup while it's still hot! Don't …

3 C-test: The boring phone call? (A true story)

Complete the text. Each blank (_) stands for one letter.

Late one evening, a girl phoned her boyfriend in his flat on the other side of town. On t*he* days wh*en* they cou*ldn*'t meet, th*ey* often h*ad* long tele*phone* conversations. Th*is* time, af*ter* she h*ad* just to*ld* him h*ow* much s*he* loved h*im*, the ph*one* suddenly we*nt* silent. Wh*at* had happ*ened*? She sp*oke* to h*im* again, b*ut* there w*as* no ans*wer*. What w*as* the mat*ter*? Could i*t* be a he*art* attack? Th*is* idea ma*de* her fe*el* so terr*ibly* worried th*at* she dec*ided* to ca*ll* the pol*ice*. Ten min*utes* later, th*ey* were out*side* the do*or* of h*is* flat. Wh*en* they ra*ng* the be*ll*, nobody ca*me*. It w*as* when th*ey* started knoc*king* and shou*ting* that t*he* young m*an* at la*st* appeared a*t* the do*or*. "What's go*ing* on?" h*e* demanded. "Wh*at*? A phone ca*ll*? Oh, God, I must have gone to sleep while she was talking!"

Tandem Activity 2

Find a partner. Then choose the left or the right side – your partner takes the other side.
Don't look at your partner's side.

A

You and your partner both have the same crossword, but some of the words are missing. Your partner's side shows the words you need and your side shows the words your partner needs. (All these words are in Unit 3.)
Help your partner to finish the crossword. First think of good clues for the words on your own side and write them down. Then take turns to ask each other and tell each other your clues.

What's the clue for 2 across?

They aren't allowed at the Youth Housing Project.

Is the first letter a 'D'?/Does it start/end with a/an ...?

Yes, it is./No, .../
Yes, it does./No, ...

Is it ...?
Do you spell it with a/an ...?

B

You and your partner both have the same crossword, but some of the words are missing. Your partner's side shows the words you need and your side shows the words your partner needs. (All these words are in Unit 3.)
Help your partner to finish the crossword. First think of good clues for the words on your own side and write them down. Then take turns to ask each other and tell each other your clues.

What's the clue for 3 down?

It's an American word for 'rubbish'.

Is the second letter an 'A'?/ Does it start/end with a/an ...?

Yes, it is./No, .../
Yes, it does./No, ...

Is it ...?
Do you spell it with a/an ...?

Focus on the early years of the US

1 Links to the past (PB p. 57/ex. 3)

a) What is shown in these photos of the US today? Write captions. *(Erwartungshorizont)*

1. *A Thanksgiving meal*

2. *The Fourth of July*

3. *Boston Harbour*

4. *A cattle ranch*

b) Explain how the photos in **a)** are linked to the history of the country.
Write a few sentences about each of them in your exercise book. *(Erwartungshorizont: S. 78)*

2 The road to freedom (PB p. 57/ex. 3)

Write down the year when people might have said these things.
Then explain who or what the **marked** pronoun refers to.

1. "Britain is fighting **them** in Europe, so now we're at war here, too."

   Year: *1754* 'Them' refers to *the French.*

2. "New taxes? No way! Not when **they** don't allow us any representation in their parliament!"

   Year: *1765* *'They' refers to the British.*

3. "Have you heard about **it** yet? Five people! No wonder everyone is so angry!"

   Year: *1770* *'It' refers to the Boston Massacre.*

4. "Well, we've started **it** now, but I don't know how we can win against the British troops."

   Year: *1775* *'It' refers to the War of Independence.*

5. "I knew we would win in the end! **He**'s a great leader!"

   Year: *1783* *'He' refers to George Washington.*

6. "Everybody else can celebrate their freedom – but what about **us**?"

   Year: *1783* *'Us' refers to slaves.*

3 A true pioneer (PB p. 58/ex. 4)

Complete the text with the correct prepositions.

More ___*than*___ anyone else, Daniel Boone (1734–1820) was responsible ___*for*___ opening up the way ___*to*___ the west. He grew up ___*in*___ Pennsylvania where he hunted and farmed. However, he was attracted ___*to/by*___ the wilderness, and ___*between*___ 1769 and 1775 he explored the Appalachians and collected information ___*about*___ paths and trails that led ___*through/over*___ the mountains. ___*Because of*___ his knowledge he was employed to mark a route which was known ___*as*___ the Wilderness Trail. ___*At*___ first the trail was not suitable ___*for*___ wagons, so people had to ride or go ___*on*___ foot. But this did not prevent thousands ___*of*___ pioneers ___*from*___ using it. While the colonies were still ___*at*___ war ___*with*___ Britain, many people were already ___*on*___ their way ___*to*___ a new life ___*in*___ the west.

4 Historical sources (PB p. 58/ex. 4)

a) What can give you information about the past? Make a list of possible sources. *(Erwartungshorizont)*

history books, *diaries, letters, old (news)papers, articles, photos and pictures,*

the internet, libraries, …

b) Read the following text. Discuss with a partner which sentences express facts and which express opinions. Underline the facts in blue and the opinions in red.

My mother's family were originally immigrants from Ireland who went west in the 1840s. They were really brave to set off on that long and difficult journey. We know quite a lot about it because Mary, one of the girls in the family, kept a diary which we still have. She also wrote letters from Oregon, which were later returned to the family. I think Mary's words say much more about that time than any history book can tell you. It is true that history books contain lots of facts, but the writers weren't actually there. So they can't possibly communicate what it was really like. We even have an old photo of Mary from the 1850s which shows her together with her husband and two children outside their little farm. They seem a bit nervous of the camera! But the details in the picture are a direct source of information about how they lived. It's strange to look at Mary, but it's a good feeling, too. It reminds me of where I come from.

c) Sum up why in the writer's opinion Mary's diary is a better source of information than a history book.

Mary's diary is a direct source of information whereas history books are often written by people who did not actually experience the events they describe.

d) Discuss whether you agree with what the writer says about history books. Give reasons.

5 Creative writing: A diary extract (PB p. 58/ex. 4)

Imagine you are Mary. Write a short extract (120–140 words) from her diary. Include both facts about the journey west, and also some of Mary's opinions. Use your exercise book.

6 There's no smoke without fire (PB p. 59/ex. 6)

a) In the past Native Americans used smoke signals to send messages about danger, and today books about how to survive in the wilderness sometimes include instructions for these signals. Match the sentence parts, find the right order for the sentences, and then write the instructions in your exercise book. *(Lösung: S. 78)*

Take the blanket away ...	Hold a blanket over the fire ...
... to collect the smoke under it.	Return the blanket ...
... in the highest place in the area.	... until the signal has been sent.
Repeat as often as necessary ...	... to stop the smoke again.
Make a fire ...	... to allow some smoke to escape.

b) Of course you cannot send a smoke signal without first making a fire!
How can you do this if you are in the wilderness and do not have any matches?
Look at the pictures and write instructions in your exercise book. (Use a dictionary for any new words you need.) Start like this: Find a dry, flat piece of wood and a ...
(Erwartungshorizont: S. 79)

7 An American history quiz (PB p. 59/ex. 7) *(Erwartungshorizont: S. 79)*

Work with a partner. Take turns to ask and answer the questions. (If you can't agree on an answer, look up the information in your book.) Write the answers down in your exercise books.

1. How many colonies did Britain have on the east coast of America?
2. Which country was Britain at war with both in Europe and in America?
3. Why were the links with Britain originally an advantage for the colonies? (two reasons)
4. What did Britain introduce in the colonies that made the people there so angry?
5. What was thrown into Boston Harbour by the angry colonists?
6. What helped to give the people in the different colonies a sense of identity as Americans?
7. What was the exact date of the Declaration of Independence?
8. Who was the American leader in the War of Independence?
9. Where did the African slaves have to work?
10. Which was the first group of people to arrive in America?
11. Why did pioneers often camp in a circle at night?
12. What happened in 1848 that made many people want to go to California?
13. Which part of America did Lewis and Clark explore?
14. Which tribe did Sacajawea originally belong to?
15. Who first called Native Americans 'Indians'?
16. Which animal did Native Americans depend on?
17. In which battle did the Sioux win their famous victory against General Custer?
18. What name was given to special pieces of land for Native Americans?

unit 4 intro

Native Americans then and now

1 Whites and Indians: 19th century attitudes (PB p. 61/ex. 2)

a) Put the sentence parts together so that they make sense. Then decide who is speaking in each case: a white person (W), or an Indian (I)? Put in the correct numbers and letters.

1. "The way they treated homesteaders that fell into their hands	2	were enough to settle our minds against them."	(W)
2. "The terrible things that happened in the Sioux rebellion	5	were things we would never have done to the four-leggeds."	(I)
3. "Before they came and took everything, we	7	makes them so crazy with greed."	(I)
4. "They fought against us so fiercely that we	6	made us think they were sick."	(I)
5. "The things they did to the buffalo	8	is a dead one."	(W)
6. "When we first saw them, their white skins	3	were able to live quite happily."	(I)
7. "We can't understand why the gold here	4	had to send out troops."	(W)
8. "The only good Indian	1	was worse than anything we had ever seen."	(W)

b) Compare your answers with a partner's, and explain your decisions.

2 Word power: What happened when the whites came (PB p. 61/ex. 2)

Read the text and fill in the crossword.

In 1830, the Indian 19 in the 20 of the United States were forced to move to land further 4, to make room for the new 1 that were being built by the whites. When it was discovered that this land was rich in 18, however, the whites' 10 for gold was so great that they made the Indians move again. After this, some of the Indians went on the 9, and attacks were made on the 3 that the whites travelled west in, and on the wooden 16 they had built for themselves. Again and again the government had to send out 8.

Although the whites signed one 2 after another, they broke them all, and the Native people 17 more and more of their land. The Sioux were a proud and 6 people, and in the Sioux rebellion of 1862, hundreds of whites were killed.

But still more settlers arrived, and railroads were built through Indian territory. Millions of buffalo were killed, but not only for their skins and 22. Many Indians 7 to death as a result; they 21 because the animals were their main source of food. "Every buffalo dead is an Indian gone," said a US Army officer.

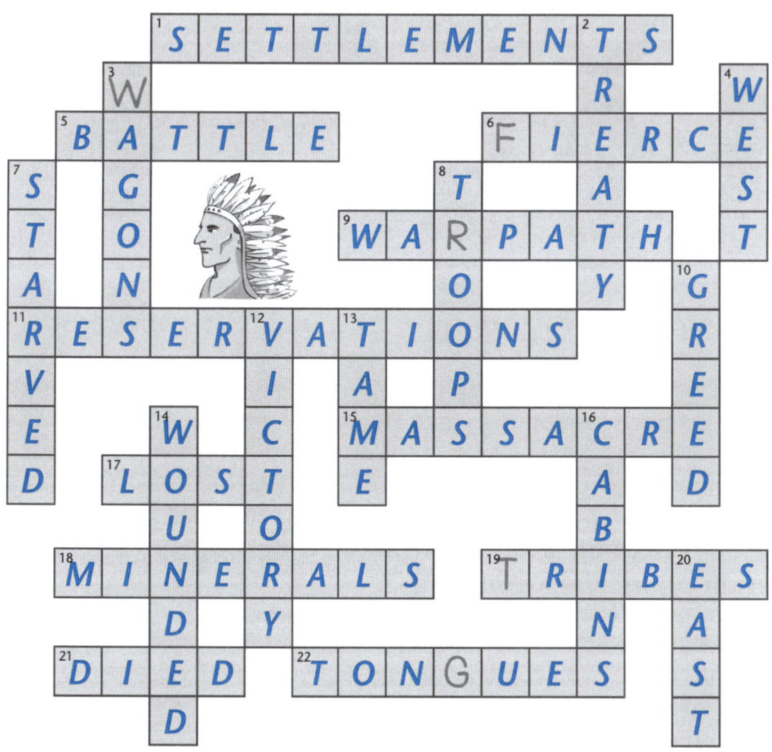

In 1876 about 12,000 Sioux Indians won their famous 12 against General Custer in the 5 of the Little Big Horn. After that, the US government did everything in its power to break the Indian people; by the 1880s most Indians were forced to live on 11, where even the wildest ones became '13'. In 1890, US soldiers killed about 200 Indian men, women and children at 14 Knee. The Indians called this a 15. It was a sign that all hopes of returning to their old way of life were gone.

1 Life in a Sioux village (PB p. 63/ex. 3)

a) Write at least six sentences to describe what you can see in this picture painted in 1830. Use ***there is/there are*** with a ***participle construction.*** The words and phrases below may be useful. *(Erwartungshorizont)*

dance • dry • hang • lie • paint • play • practise • ride • sit • stand • work

buffalo skins • horses • pictures and symbols • pieces of buffalo meat •

in the background • on the left/right

There are three tipis standing quite close together. At the front of the picture there's a large buffalo skin fixed to the ground, and there are *two women sitting/working on it. There are two men standing outside the tipis. There are pictures and symbols painted on the sides of the tipis. Near the tipis there are some pieces of buffalo meat drying in the sun. In the background there is someone riding a horse, and on the right there are two people sitting on another horse. Near them there are children dancing, and on the left there are two other children practising archery/with bows and arrows.*

b) Find a partner and check each other's work. Talk about any details you missed.
Example: "Look, here's a detail you didn't notice. There's/There are …

2 Participles as adjectives (PB p. 63/ex. 3)

a) You already know a lot of participles that are used as adjectives.
(For example, 'surprising' and 'surprised' both come from the verb 'to surprise'.)
Complete these sentences with the correct ***present*** or ***past participle forms***.

1. We saw a terribly *exciting* western yesterday! **(excite)**
2. Some of the battle scenes were a bit *frightening*. In fact, at one point Emma was so *horrified* that she closed her eyes! **(frighten • horrify)**
3. At first we were quite *surprised* because the Indians were actually presented as the heroes! But it was a bit *disappointing* to notice that all the Indian roles were played by whites. **(surprise • disappoint)**
4. Emma found the landscape *fascinating*. She was especially *interested* in the scenes of Arizona, because she had been there once. **(fascinate • interest)**

b) Now write sentences of your own with the same verbs – using the ***participle forms*** you did not make in **a)**. Write in your exercise book.

3 More about the Plains Indians (PB p. 63/ex. 3) *(Lösung: S. 79)*

Use ***participle constructions*** to rephrase these sentences. In some cases, you will need to use the participle (as an adjective) before the noun. Write in your exercise book.

1. The Indians **who lived on the Great Plains** had a great love and respect for nature and everything **that belonged to the natural world.**

2. They believed that all things **that lived** would return to the earth again in time.

3. This idea of the 'circle of life' **that led from birth to death** meant that the circle became an important symbol.

4. They saw this circle (or cycle[1]) in the sun **that rose and went down again each day** and in the seasons **as they changed.**

5. The tipis **that were made by the women** were circular, and there were often circular designs **they had painted on the sides.**

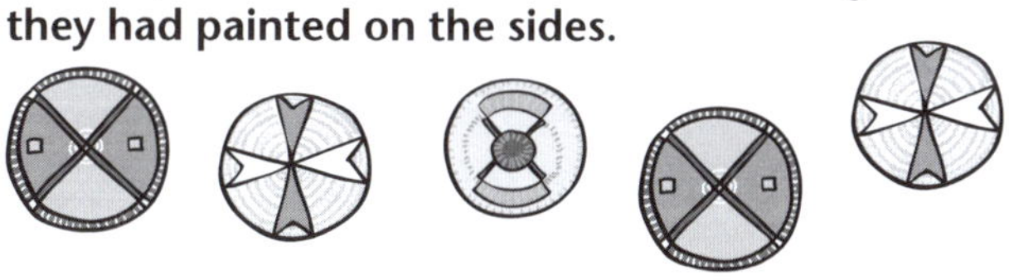

6. The clothes **(with beautiful decorations) that were worn** for tribal festivals sometimes also showed a circle **that stood out as a religious symbol.**

7. Almost all Indian tribes believed that a god **that they called 'the Great Spirit[2]'** had created the whole of nature.

8. They thought that everything **that had been created on the earth** was naturally dependent on everything else, and that there was a spirit **that was hidden deep in every animal, every mountain, every river.**

[1]['saɪkl] – Zyklus • [2]['spɪrɪt] – Geist

11 4 Listening: Native Americans on horseback (PB p. 63/ex. 3)

a) You are going to hear another part of the radio interview with Sam Kenyon. First listen. Then read through the sentences, before you listen again. Tick ✔ the correct statements. Sometimes more than one may be right.

1. The Indian Wars
- [ ] **a)** started in 1846.
- [x] **b)** were between the American Army and groups of Native Americans.
- [ ] **c)** were fought by white settlers against the Indians.

2. The Native Americans
- [ ] **a)** had horses even before the Spanish came to America.
- [ ] **b)** bought their horses from the Spanish.
- [x] **c)** took horses from the Spanish at the time of the rebellion in 1680.

3. As cowboys, the Native Americans
- [x] **a)** had a big advantage because they knew the country so well.
- [x] **b)** were well able to survive because they were so tough.
- [ ] **c)** never worked in teams with whites.

4. Cowboys who met Indians on the way north
- [ ] **a)** were not allowed to ride through their reservations.
- [x] **b)** usually traded with them.
- [x] **c)** were often able to get food and other goods from them.

b) Now answer these questions in your exercise book. *(Erwartungshorizont: S. 79)*

1. What do you find out from Sam Kenyon about the life of a typical cowboy?
2. Why could it be an advantage to have a Native American in a team of cowboys? Give at least two reasons.

Klamath Tribes fight to win back lands

1 From the 19th century to the present day (PB p. 65/ex. 2)

Complete this text with the right combination of words.

acres • arrival • chance • rates • way • years + of + history • land • life • settlers • unemployment • success

The Klamaths' problems began in the 19th century with the ___*arrival of settlers*___ from Europe. At that time the tribe still controlled 22 million ___*acres of land*___. Even when the US government took away most of this territory, they managed to keep up their traditional ___*way of life*___. But when the tribe was 'terminated' in 1954, they had little ___*chance of success*___ and soon there were high ___*rates of unemployment*___, alcoholism and suicide. Now the Klamaths are again officially recognized, and although they cannot reverse 150 ___*years of history*___, they still hope to get some of their land back.

2 Should the Klamaths get their land back? (PB p. 65/ ex. 3)

a) Complete the text with suitable ***participles*** (present or past). Choose from the verbs in the boxes.

do | face | fear | give | hope | live | respect

1. The Klamath Tribes are fighting for their land, ___*hoping*___ also to put right the damage ___*done*___ over the years to the environment. Many of the animals once ___*living*___ on their territory are now in danger of dying out. Naturally, when ___*faced*___ by the idea of losing their land, non-native landowners worry about their future. Companies are against the Tribes' plans, ___*fearing*___ that their profits will suffer. Some environmentalists, although ___*respecting*___ the Native Americans' traditions, are afraid that land ___*given*___ back to the Tribes might no longer be protected by US laws.

agree | believe | know | own | speak

2. "While ___*agreeing*___ that the Indians have been treated badly," they argue, "we still don't think that public lands should be returned to them." When ___*speaking*___ at a recent meeting, many non-natives ___*owning*___ land on the old reservation territory said that the land was simply too valuable to the people of the US. But the Klamaths have no reason to change their minds, ___*knowing*___ that their rights to the land are thousands of years old, and ___*believing*___ that it was originally given freely to them by the Great Spirit.

b) Should the Klamaths' land be returned to them? Explain the arguments for and against in a few sentences. Then give your own opinion, while trying to see the problem from both sides.

c) With a partner, discuss the arguments you wrote down in **b)**. Do you both agree?

3 Christopher Columbus (PB p. 65/ex. 4)

a) Read the text and mark all the ***participle constructions*** you can find in colour. (You may use different colours for the different forms.)

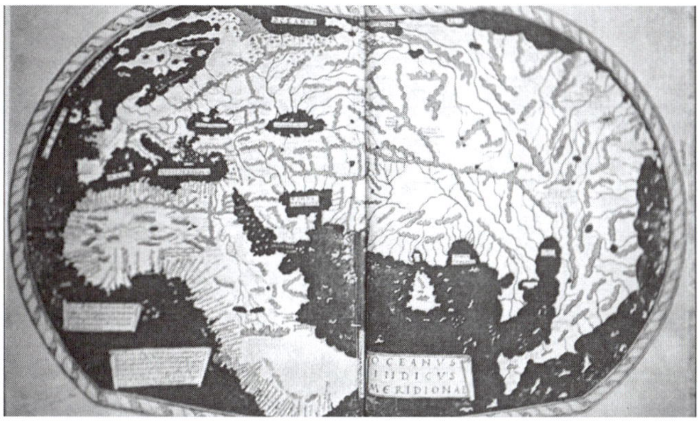

Maps of the world drawn in the 15th century show a large mass of land shaped a bit like a pancake and surrounded by an area of ocean. Believing that the earth actually was as flat as a pancake, sailors in those days were afraid of going too far out to sea beyond the coasts of the world they knew. They especially feared the sea now called the Atlantic Ocean (but known in those days as the Sea of Gloom[1]), imagining that if they sailed out too far, they would come to the edge of the world and fall off!

But Cristoforo Colombo, known to us as Christopher Columbus, was one of the few people that believed the earth was round, having spent a lot of time with astronomers[2] and mathematicians[3] who were beginning to agree on this new theory. He argued that if the theory was correct, ships sailing far enough west across the Atlantic would get to Asia in the end. However, he needed someone to sponsor him. Queen Isabella of Spain, though refusing to agree at first, was finally persuaded, and on the evening of 3 August 1492 Columbus's ship, the *Santa Maria,* accompanied by two others, left Spain with forty men on board.

Having sailed through August and September without any sight of land, the crews began to get very worried. Knowing how many miles they had travelled (actually much further than he had expected!), and fearing that panic would break out among the men, Columbus promised he would turn back if they were still in open sea 48 hours later. On the night of 11 October, he prayed to God with all his heart and soul. Amazingly, on the following day land was in sight! They had reached the island later known as San Salvador in the Bahamas.

Though now remembered as the first European to discover the New World, till his dying day Columbus continued to believe that the land he had sailed to was part of Asia.

[1] [glu:m] – Dunkelheit, Schwermut •
[2] [ə'strɒnəməz] •
[3] [ˌmæθmə'tɪʃnz] •

b) Now work with a partner. Decide together how the constructions you have marked can be rewritten so that the meaning is expressed without ***participles***. Then discuss what advantage the use of ***participle constructions*** in a text like this may have.

1 Homesteaders on the Plains (PB p. 66/ex. 1) *(Erwartungshorizont: S. 79)*

Read the information given here. Then, with the help of the tips on page 66 of your book, write an interesting text about life on the Plains. Use your exercise book.

The first settlers crossed the Great Plains quickly. The land did not seem good for farming. So they did not want to live there.

1850s and 1860s: This attitude began to change. The railroad companies wanted to attract new settlers. They advertised land and sold it cheaply. 1862: The US government decided to give land away! Settlers were allowed 160 acres of land free; they only had to agree to build a house and live there for five years. The government made 2.5 million acres available.

The first homesteaders travelled in wagons. Then the railroads were built. People began to come by train. Most came as families. They arrived on the Plains full of hope. They had read the wonderful adverts. Farmers from the eastern states had brought seeds and farming tools. But they got a shock when they started to work. Their seeds did not grow, and their tools were not suitable for the Great Plains.

The main problems

- The weather: Often very windy, but terribly hot in summer. Snow storms in winter. Heavy rain, often followed by weeks of very dry weather.
- Fires: Fires were spread by the wind. They could ruin all crops.

- No fences: No wood. Wild animals or cattle ruined the crops.
- Very few trees: Homes had to be built out of dried earth.
- Too little water: Not enough for wheat to grow. The hard earth was difficult to plough.
- Grasshoppers[1]: Sometimes millions of them came. They could eat all the crops in a few hours.

Life was hard. Impossible to keep houses clean – dusty in dry weather, wet when it rained. No toilets or clean water. Dirty conditions caused illness. There were few doctors. Children often died from diseases. Many women died in childbirth.

[1] [ˈɡrɑːsˌhɒpəz] – Heuschrecken

2 Formal enough? (PB p. 67/ex. 2)

a) Look at these phrases, then decide which of them would be suitable for a formal letter to the editor of a newspaper or magazine.
Mark each phrase: ✔ (formal enough), ✘ (too informal), ! (rude).

1. ✔ As far as … is concerned, …
2. ! This is bullshit!
3. ✔ It must be pointed out that …
4. ✔ Readers may be interested to learn that …
5. ✘ I've simply got to tell you that …
6. ! What the hell does … know about …
7. ✘ It's just not OK to say that …
8. ! Only a jerk would argue that …
9. ✔ Unfortunately I disagree with …
10. ✔ Although it may be true that …
11. ✔ As far as I am aware, …
12. ! I want to say something about that damn silly article on …

b) Compare your answers with a partner's. Then discuss how (or whether) the phrases you agree are not suitable could be rewritten and improved. *(Erwartungshorizont: S. 79)*

1 Is that correct? (PB p. 71/ex. 1)

a) How well did you understand the story 'Ta-Na-E-Ka' on pages 68–71 of your book?
Decide if these statements are true (✔), false (✘), or if no information is given in the text (–).

1. [–] Mary's grandfather made his own clothes and shoes.
2. [✘] Mary's teacher was against the ritual.
3. [✔] Ta-Na-E-Ka wasn't such a tough test of endurance as it had been in the past.
4. [✔] Before the ritual began, Mary borrowed five dollars, promising to babysit in return.
5. [–] Ernie had lost two of his fingers during the Second World War.
6. [✘] He and Mary both agreed that the Ta-Na-E-Ka ritual was crazy.
7. [–] Mary felt guilty when she saw poor Roger.
8. [✘] Her grandfather had survived on orange berries during his own Ta-Na-E-Ka.

b) Now correct the false statements.
Write in your exercise book.
(Erwartungshorizont: S. 79)

c) Talk about the statements marked (–) with a partner. How likely or unlikely do they seem to be?

2 Creative writing: Roger's survival test (PB p. 71/ex. 3) *(Erwartungshorizont: S. 79)*

Look at the pictures and then tell the story of what happened to Roger after he had said goodbye to Mary. Remember to describe his thoughts and feelings, too. Write about 150–200 words in your exercise book.

⟨3⟩ The American west: A talk (PB p. 71/ex. 3)

a) First choose a topic that you and the others in your group find interesting. Here are some ideas:

- Indian tribes, their traditions and beliefs
- The life of a cowboy in the 19th century
- How 'wild' was the west really?
- Native Americans today
- Why people went west – and where they settled
- …

b) Then search for material on your chosen subject. Collect information, including pictures, maps, etc., and prepare a talk together. Make sure everybody has a role to play in preparing and presenting the talk. (Remember to include suitable visual elements, such as transparencies, diagrams, etc. Perhaps you can also prepare a handout for your audience.)

4 Different types of text (PB p. 71/ex. 3)

a) First read the texts in the boxes. Then read the extracts below and decide which box goes with which extract. Put in the correct letter.

A	B	C	D	E
Here, Francis Parkman, from a rich Boston family, describes his journey west with a friend in 1846.	This text is taken from a history book called *Native peoples of North America.*	This is from a short story written by Louis L'Amour.	A Blackfeet Indian chief speaks to the whites who want him to sign one of the first land treaties.	This description, from a DVD catalogue, is about 'Hondo', an American movie made in 1953.

D Our land is more valuable than your money. It will last forever. As long as the sun shines and the waters flow, this land will be here to give life to men and animals. We cannot sell the lives of men and animals; therefore we cannot sell this land.

It was given to us by the Great Spirit. We cannot sell it because it does not belong to us.

C White in the face, she stood in the door of her cabin with a shotgun in her hands. Beside the door was a Winchester, and on the table inside the house were two Walker Colts. Her heart beat heavily.

Outside the cabin were twelve Apaches, and one of the Indians had lifted his hand.

E In this classic western, John Wayne's relationship with ranch wife Geraldine Page, whose husband has left her, is complicated by trouble with the Indians.

The natural beauty of the landscape comes over perfectly in this brilliant movie.

B From the 1850s, many white settlers made the dangerous journey across the Plains in their covered wagons. They travelled to new homes in Oregon and California along a route called the Oregon Trail. This passed through the southern part of Sioux territory.

The Sioux were one of the proudest and the strongest of the Indian nations.

A After many adventures, we finally reached Fort Laramie. It was there that we first met with the Dakota Indians. The Dakota lived in a vast territory from the St. Peter River to the Rocky Mountains.

Most evenings Shaw and I visited the Dakota camp of Chief Old Smoke.

b) Now read these 'extra' sentences. Decide which extracts they go with and write them in.

- The natural beauty of the landscape comes over perfectly in this brilliant movie.
- It was given to us by the Great Spirit. We cannot sell it because it does not belong to us.
- Most evenings Shaw and I visited the Dakota camp of Chief Old Smoke.
- The Sioux were one of the proudest and the strongest of the Indian nations.
- Outside the cabin were twelve Apaches, and one of the Indians had lifted his hand.

c) Think about the intention behind each of these texts. Why do you think they were written?

Text E: to try to persuade people to buy something.
Text C: to provide readers with entertainment.
Text D: to try to make people understand different values.
Text A: to describe authentic personal experiences.
Text B: to inform readers about important events in the past.

5 A summary (PB p. 71/ex. 3)

Think of a story, for example, from a book or a film you have enjoyed recently. Write a summary of it in your exercise book, using the present tense.

6 Mediation/Listening: Chief Joseph and the Nez Perce[1] (PB p. 72/ex. 4)

a) Lena Schubert is in America with her parents. One day they visit a Native American reservation, where Julia, an American guide, tells the story of Chief Joseph. Take notes while you listen.

b) Some other German tourists have not understood everything. How can Lena explain things to them in German? Use your exercise book. *(Erwartungshorizont: S. 79)*

1. Das war sehr interessant, aber ich hab' nicht alles verstanden. Warum hat Julia Lewis und Clark erwähnt? Die waren doch nicht an dem Land der Nez Perce interessiert, oder?
2. Das Wort ‚treaty' habe ich verstanden. Eine Art Abkommen also. Aber worum ging es dabei, und warum haben die Weißen ihr Wort nicht gehalten?
3. Joseph hat also nachgegeben, weil er keine andere Wahl hatte. Trotzdem hat Julia etwas von Soldaten erzählt: ‚US troops'. Warum wurden sie denn eingesetzt?
4. Warum ist es den Indianern nicht gelungen; über die Grenze nach Kanada zu fliehen?
5. Mir ist leider nicht ganz klar, was mit Joseph und seinem Volk nach der Niederlage geschah.

[1] ['nez,pɜːs]

7 Mediation: Which western? (PB p. 72/ex. 5)

ZDF 20.15 Rio Bravo

Ein Top-Western von legendärer Coolness

Tarantinos Lieblings-Western: Kultfilm mit John Wayne und Dean Martin
Howard Hawks drehte diesen Klassiker als Antwort auf „Zwölf Uhr mittags". Dort bittet Sheriff Gary Cooper brave Bürger um Hilfe. Bei Hawks macht Sheriff Chance (John Wayne) klar, dass er die Killer eines Viehbarons notfalls allein erledigt. Seine Unterstützer sind ein Säufer (Dean Martin), ein Opa (Walter Brennan), eine Zockerin (Angie Dickinson) und ein Greenhorn (Ricky Nelson) …

O: Rio Bravo; USA 1959
R: Howard Hanks

HUMOR	ANSPRUCH	ACTION	SPANNUNG
✶	✶✶	✶✶	✶✶

ARTE 20.40 Die gefürchteten Vier

Cooler Westernthriller voller Ironie und Action

Dreifach Oscar-nominierter Western mit Burt Lancaster
Pistolero Fardan (Lee Marvin), Sprengmeister Dolworth (Burt Lancaster), Bogenschütze Sharp und Pferdeexperte Ehrengard: Diese Profis beauftragt Rinderbaron Grant, seine Frau (Claudia Cardinale) aus den Händen des mexikanischen Banditen Raza (Jack Palance) zu retten. In Razas Lager gibt es eine Überraschung … Witzig-actionreiches Spiel mit Western-Stereotypen.

O: The Professionals; USA 1966
R: Richard Brooks

HUMOR	ANSPRUCH	ACTION	SPANNUNG
✶	✶✶	✶✶	✶✶

a) Imagine you have a British friend staying with you. Which of the two westerns do you want to watch together? Briefly explain in English what each film is about, and decide which one you would suggest watching. Say why. *(Erwartungshorizont)*

'Rio Bravo' is about a sheriff (played by John Wayne) who says he can deal with the killers of a big cattle owner on his own if necessary. He is helped by a drinker, an old man and two other people, one of them a woman. In 'The Professionals' another big cattle owner, called Grant, employs four different people to save his wife from a Mexican gangster, called Raza. But there's a surprise waiting for them in Raza's camp. Both films sound equally exciting and fun to watch. Perhaps I'd prefer to watch 'The Professionals' because of the stereotypes and also it might be more interesting because there is a surprise.

b) Talk to a partner about the two films, and discuss your reasons for preferring the one you have chosen.

1 Word power (PB p. 73/ex. 1)

a) Decide which groups these words belong to. Find a heading for the third and fourth group.

alcoholism • crime • director • feature film • firm • homesteader • income • invest • pioneer • poverty • producer • profit • screen • settlement • unemployment • wagon

1. Social problems	2. Entertainment industry	3. *19th century America*	4. *Business world*
alcoholism	*director*	*homesteader*	*firm*
crime	*feature film*	*pioneer*	*income*
poverty	*producer*	*settlement*	*invest*
unemployment	*screen*	*wagon*	*profit*

b) Choose two words from each group, and use them in sentences to show you understand their meaning.

c) Work with a partner. Which of you can think of most words to add to the four groups?

2 The stagecoach (PB p. 73/ex. 2) *(Lösung: S. 80)*

Rewrite the sentences in your exercise book, using ***participles*** wherever suitable.

1. A stagecoach in the west travelled for up to fifteen hours a day, and made journeys of 40 to 60 miles in the summer months.
2. In hundreds of cowboy films, stagecoaches that cross the dusty western landscape are stopped by outlaws or Indians.
3. In reality, the stagecoaches that were used in the west had little to do with the lives of cowboys.
4. However, because they knew passengers usually had money or valuable goods with them, outlaws did attack stagecoaches quite often.
5. In 1877, the coaches that belonged to the Wells Fargo company were attacked 200 times in a single month!
6. But soon the railroads that were built across the continent put an end to the days of stagecoach travel, as they made journeys quicker, safer and more comfortable.

3 Mixed bag: Cowgirls (PB p. 73/ex. 3)

In the 19th century most women looked *after* children and worked *at* home. Women's long *skirts/dresses* made it *impossible* for them to *do* the same sort of work *as* men. But in the west things *were* often different. The women *who/that* travelled in wagons with *their* families often worked just *like* the men. *When* they settled, some *of* them managed ranches *while* their husbands were away or after they *had* died. A few even put *on* men's clothes and joined the cowboys on horseback. This sometimes *made* them unpopular, and the men did not *know* what to think *of* them, because these cowgirls did not *look/behave* like the women *they* were used to. There were even *one* or two women that ran *away* from home and actually joined outlaw gangs.

General revision

1 Agreeing and disagreeing (PB p. 74/ex. 2))

Use short answers to agree or disagree. Read everything first, before you decide on the right reaction.

1. "My father goes mad if I get home late!" – "*So does mine*. He's terribly strict about things like that."
2. "We don't like Chinese food much." – "*But we do*. We're always getting stuff at the Chinese takeaway!"
3. "We've got quite a big garden."– "*So have we*. My parents are always complaining about all the work it makes."
4. "I can't play football very well." – "*Nor/Neither can I*. But I'm quite good at basketball."
5. "I really must go home now!" – "*So must I*. I've got so much homework to do."
6. "I'll always remember what a great time we had yesterday!" – "*So will I*. It was fantastic!"
7. "Our dog never eats meat out of a tin." – "*Ours does*. Opening a tin's so convenient!"
8. "I wouldn't much like to work in a hospital." – "*Nor/Neither would I*. I can't stand the sight of blood!"

2 Using emphasis (PB p. 74/ex. 2)

Find suitable ways of replying to what these people say. Use the different types of emphasis given.

1. *John:* I hate it when my brother takes my things without asking!

   You: My sister's just the same! She *'s always taking my things*. **(always)**
2. *Sam:* I need a new computer, not a TV.

   You: With me it's the opposite. *What I need is a new TV*. **(What)**
3. *Julia:* I don't think Emma wants to come to the cinema with us.

   You: You're wrong! *She does want to come with us*. **(do)**
4. *Lucy:* Tom wasn't trying to get off with me at that party. George was!

   You: I didn't realize! So *it was George that was trying to get off with you*. **(it was)**
5. *Anna:* My mum complains so much. I wish she'd stop!

   You: She sounds like my father. *He's always complaining*! **(always)**
6. *Adam:* Great that you won that competition! I bet you're pleased.

   You: Yeah! *I'm/I feel really pleased*. **(really)**

3 What would you say? (PB p. 75/ex. 4)

Express these ideas differently. Make suitable sentences with ***make*** or ***let*** + ***object*** + ***infinitive***, or ***have*** + ***object*** + ***past participle***.

1. I don't want to repaint my bedroom walls myself.

   I want *to have them painted/have it done professionally*.

2. I'm not going to go to university when I leave school. Dad can't force me!

   Dad *can't make me go to university if I don't want to*.

3. Whenever I ask Brad if I can borrow books or CDs, he always says 'no'.

   Brad *never lets me borrow his books or CDs*.

4. Has nobody come to repair your TV yet? Why don't you ask someone to deal with it?

   Why *don't you have it repaired*?

5. Emma doesn't mind if her dog sleeps in her room, but it isn't allowed to lie on her bed.

   Emma *lets her dog sleep in her room, but doesn't let it lie on her bed*.

4 Treasure Island (PB p. 75/ex. 5)

Fill in the gaps with suitable ***participle forms***. Choose from the verbs given.

call | hide | love | stay | write

1. 'Treasure Island', an adventure story *written* by Robert Louis Stevenson, was published in 1883. The book, *loved* by readers of all ages, immediately made Stevenson famous. The narrator is a boy *called* Jim Hawkins, whose mother keeps an inn somewhere on the English coast. Billy Bones, an old seaman *staying* at the inn, has a map that shows the exact location of the treasure *hidden* on a faraway island by an old pirate.

beat | excite | excite | help | know | take | work

2. *Knowing* that Bones has the map, a group of his evil old pirate 'friends' come to the inn one night. But by this time Bones has died, and Jim, *helped* by his mother, has found the map. Jim takes the map to Squire[1] Trelawney and greatly *excited* by the hope of finding the treasure, the Squire and his friend Dr Livesey set off for the island in the ship *Hispaniola*, *taking* Jim with them. Some of the crew are reliable men but most are actually old pirates *working* for Long John Silver, the one-legged ship's cook. Their plan to take over the ship and kill the Squire and his friends is discovered by Jim, and after a series of *exciting* adventures on the island, the treasure is found and the pirates *beaten*.

[1] [skwaɪə] – Gutsherr

13 5 Listening: The Fair Trade movement (PB p. 77/ex. 10)

a) Jessica is talking to her new boyfriend, Daniel. Listen to their conversation. Then look at the sentences below before listening again.
Mark each statement, either as 'correct' (✔), 'false' (✘) or 'not given' (–).

✘ 1. Jessica and Daniel are going swimming on Saturday.
✔ 2. Jessica's mother works in a shop called 'One World'.
✘ 3. She has been working there for almost three years.
– 4. Jessica first started helping in the shop a couple of weeks ago.
✔ 5. The Fair Trade movement tries to help farmers and workers in developing countries.
✔ 6. The idea behind it is to pay them a fair price for their products.
✘ 7. Oxfam started selling Fair Trade goods only a few years ago.
– 8. Mexican coffee growers still work for poverty level wages.
✘ 9. You can't buy Fair Trade products in British supermarkets.
✘ 10. There are sheep on the big plantations in some places.
✔ 11. Even on Fair Trade plantations, workers sometimes aren't paid as well as they should be.
– 12. Daniel isn't going to buy Fair Trade products, because he feels they cost too much.

Fair Trade coffee grower

Fair Trade tea grower

b) Would you buy products with the Fair Trade label? Give reasons for your decision, based on the information you got from the conversation between Jessica and Daniel. Write about 100 words in your exercise book.
(Erwartungshorizont: S. 80)

6 Mediation: Retiring at the age of 100 (PB p. 77/ex. 10) *(Erwartungshorizont: S. 80)*

Tobias's American friend Mark is staying with Tobias's family in Germany. When Mark sees this article in the newspaper, he wants Tobias to explain to him what it is about. Read the article carefully. Then, without translating it word for word, give the main facts in English.

GESELLSCHAFT **Amerikaner war in 72 Arbeitsjahren nie krank**
Mit 100 Jahren in den Ruhestand

LOS ANGELES ■ Ein 100 Jahre alter Amerikaner ist nach 72 Jahren am selben Arbeitsplatz in den verdienten Ruhestand getreten. An seinem Geburtstag in dieser Woche erschien Arthur Winston zum letzten Mal bei den städtischen Verkehrsbetrieben in Los Angeles (Kalifornien), wo er für die Wartung und Reinigung der Busse zuständig war.

Der rüstige Mann, der keinen einzigen Arbeitstag wegen Krankheit versäumte, fehlte nur ein einziges Mal – das war im Jahr 1988, als seine Frau starb. Er habe nicht geraucht und keinen Alkohol getrunken, gab Winston als Grund für seine Gesundheit und Langlebigkeit an. Der damalige US-Präsident Bill Clinton hatte den Afroamerikaner im Jahr 1996 als „Angestellten des Jahrhunderts" ausgezeichnet.

Eigentlich wollte er als Mechaniker Busse reparieren, aber wegen seiner Hautfarbe sei ihm diese Tätigkeit in den 30er Jahren verwehrt worden, sagte Winston. Bei seinem ersten Job als Hausmeister in Los Angeles im Jahr 1924 habe er 41 Cent in der Stunde verdient. dpa

7 Work in the 18th and 19th centuries (PB p. 77/ex. 10)

Complete the text, using suitable words from the box on the right. There are more words than you will need.

craftsmen • deliver • forced • growing • grown • had • Industrial • Industry • life • living • many • mechanics • much • near • nearly • of • sent • than • that • wealthy • what • with • workshops

Before the *Industrial* Revolution, nearly everything *that* most people needed, such as clothes, tools, bread and beer, was made in their own villages. Only the *wealthy* had books, furniture, silverware and such fine things *sent* from London. But after the new 'manufacturing' towns had been built *near* the coalmines and industry, *many* people worked together in factories, instead of at home with their families. *Living* conditions were miserable. As the population was *growing*, there were plenty of workers wanting jobs, so wages were low and hours of work very long. Of course, not all the working people of England were suddenly *forced* into factories and slums. Most of the skilled trades continued as before in the small *workshops* of the towns and villages: the clock-makers, coach-builders and other *craftsmen* were able to do their work far better *than* machines. The many servants in big houses and inns, the farmworkers and the fishermen *had* never heard *of* the dark, dirty factories in the North of England.

From: R.J. Unstead, Looking at history

8 C-test: The schoolboy mayor[1] (PB p. 77/ex. 10)

Put in the missing letters to complete the text.

In November 2005, Michael Sessions, an 18-year-old schoolboy from Hillsdale, Michigan, became the youngest mayor ever elected in the USA. Just li*ke* any ot*her* American teen*ager*, Michael st*ill* continued t*o* go t*o* his hi*gh* school ev*ery* day un*til* 3 pm, b*ut* the ne*xt* three ho*urs* were sp*ent* on h*is* job a*s* mayor. Af*ter* he w*as* elected, h*e* and h*is* friends celeb*rated* his vic*tory* with so*ft* drinks (n*o* alcohol!). "Obvi*ously*, the peo*ple* of Hill*sdale* took m*e* seriously," h*e* proudly to*ld* the lo*cal* newspaper. "A l*ot* of ol*der* people rea*lly* enjoyed tal*king* to m*e* during t*he* campaign. Yo*ung* people co*uld* relate t*o* me. I'*m* really go*ing* to lo*ve* this j*ob*!" Some peo*ple* think Mic*hael* may b*e* the Pres*ident* of t*he* United Sta*tes* one d*ay*. But that won't be possible until he is 35.

[1] [meə] – Bürgermeister

The Golden State

1 What do you know about California? (PB p. 78/ex. 1)

a) Complete the key to the map with the correct names from the box on the right.
Use the maps at the back of your book to check your answers.

1. *Lassen Peak*
2. *Sacramento*
3. *San Francisco*
4. *Silicon Valley*
5. *Yosemite National Park*
6. *Mount Whitney*
7. *Death Valley*
8. *Los Angeles*
9. *San Diego*

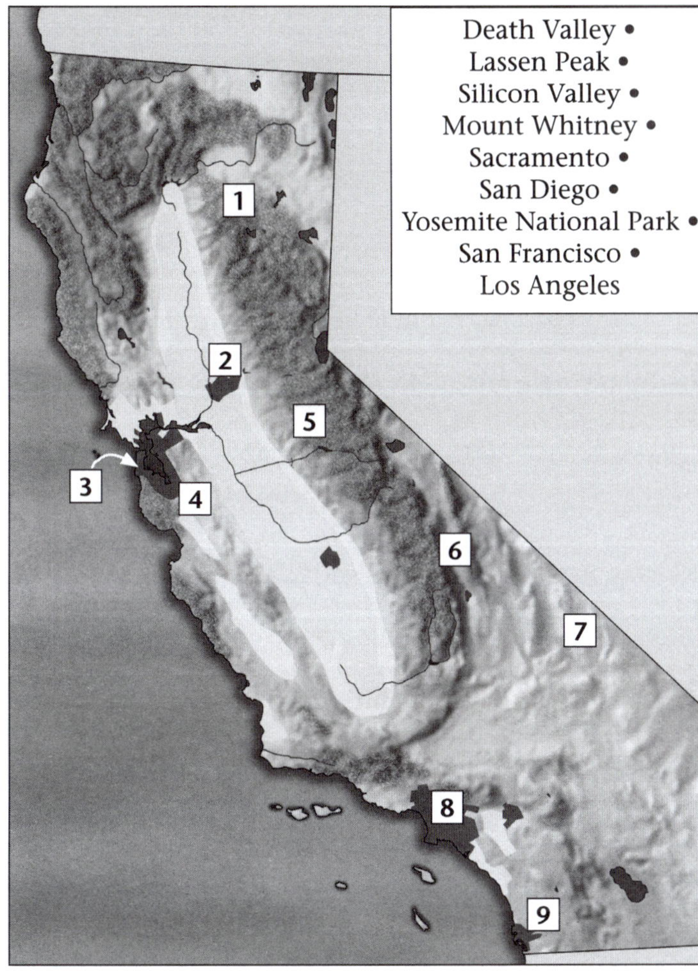

Death Valley •
Lassen Peak •
Silicon Valley •
Mount Whitney •
Sacramento •
San Diego •
Yosemite National Park •
San Francisco •
Los Angeles

b) Make a quiz about California.
Write ten questions in your exercise book and then test your partner.
(Erwartungshorizont: S. 80)
Example: What started in California in 1848?

2 Odd one out (PB p. 79/ex. 2)

Underline the odd word out. Then write a note to explain what the other words have in common.

1. milk – cheese – <u>wine</u> – butter: *dairy products*
2. <u>smog</u> – desert – mountain – plain: *landscape features*
3. movie – trash – fries – <u>holiday</u>: *American English words*
4. timber – water – <u>computers</u> – gold: *natural resources*
5. figure – <u>feature</u> – total – sum: *words about numbers*
6. tourism – films – agriculture – <u>studios</u>: *industries*
7. drought – <u>soil</u> – landslide – earthquake: *natural hazards*
8. <u>cause</u> – danger – risk – hazard: *words with similar meaning*

Skills: Interpreting diagrams

1 Language statistics (PB p. 80/ex. 1)

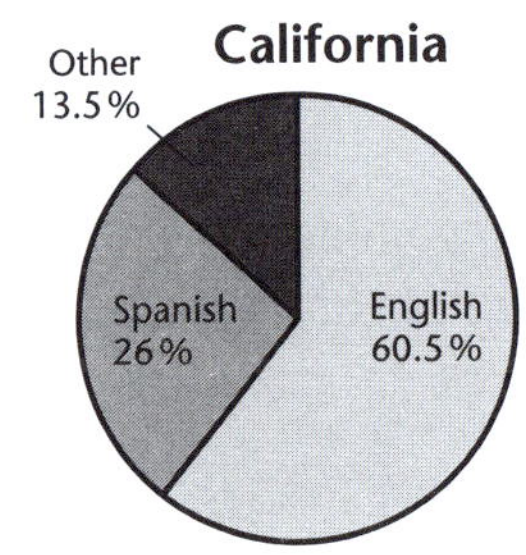

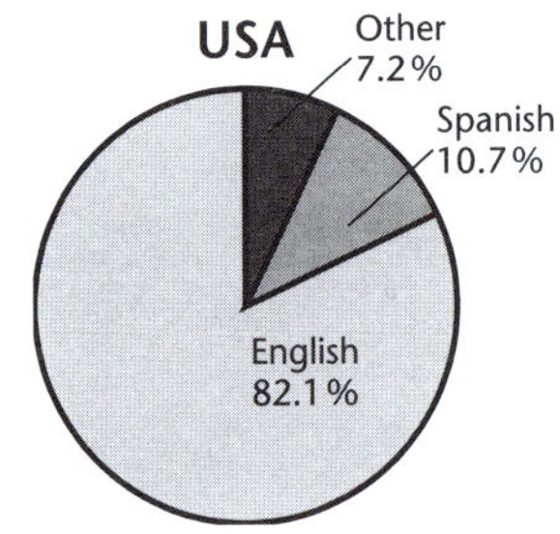

The diagrams on the right show what languages Americans speak at home. Complete the text below.

The two ___*pie*___ charts show that both in the US and in California alone the ___*majority*___ of people speak English. However, in ___*comparison*___ with the rest of the country, California has a smaller ___*percentage*___ of the population that speak English at home. ___*More*___ than ___*four*___ fifths of all Americans belong to this group, whereas in California the number falls to less ___*than*___ two ___*thirds*___. On the other hand California has almost two and a ___*half*___ times as ___*many*___ Spanish speakers. Twenty-six ___*percent*___ of Californians speak Spanish at home, but in the whole US it is the first language for ___*less*___ than eleven people in a hundred. The diagrams also ___*give/show*___ statistics for other languages. In California the figure is thirteen ___*point*___ five percent, almost ___*twice/double*___ the figure for the US.

2 A circle of success (PB p. 80/ex. 3)

a) Silicon Valley is an example of how new inventions can lead to a 'circle of success'. Study the boxes on the right. They are part of a diagram that shows how this happens. How do you think the different developments are connected? Draw arrows to show the links and complete the diagram. (You may want to draw more than one arrow to or from a box.)

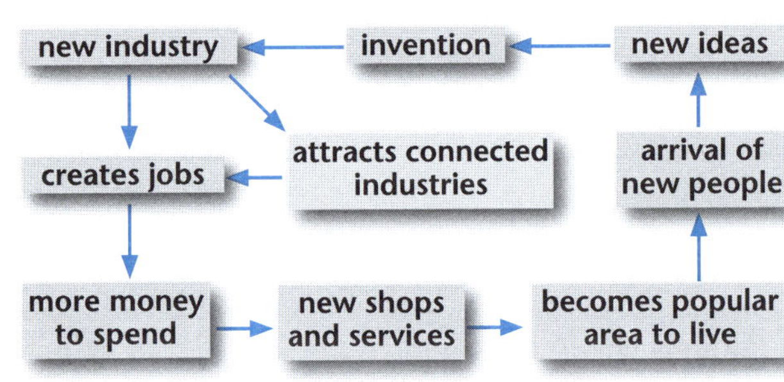

b) Work with a partner and compare the links you found. If you created different links, explain why.

c) Write a paragraph in your exercise book to explain the information in your diagram.
(Erwartungshorizont: S. 80)

3 Weather information (PB p. 80/ex. 4)

a) Look at these weather charts for San Francisco and Los Angeles. Sum up in two or three sentences in your exercise book what information the statistics give you about the climate in the two cities.
(Erwartungshorizont: S. 80)

San Francisco	Jan	Feb	Mar	Apr	May	Jun	Jul	Aug	Sep	Oct	Nov	Dec
average max. temp.	13.5	15.5	16.0	16.7	17.0	17.8	18.1	18.6	20.3	20.3	17.0	13.5
average rainfall (mm)	111.9	77.4	77.9	34.2	10.1	4.0	0.6	1.7	6.6	28.3	72.8	90.8
Los Angeles	**Jan**	**Feb**	**Mar**	**Apr**	**May**	**Jun**	**Jul**	**Aug**	**Sep**	**Oct**	**Nov**	**Dec**
average max. temp.	18.7	18.8	18.6	19.6	20.5	22.1	24.0	24.7	24.7	23.5	21.2	18.8
average rainfall (mm)	70.4	60.9	51.2	19.6	3.3	1.2	0.5	2.3	4.7	7.2	37.6	42.8

b) Think how you could improve the presentation of the statistics in **a)** so that it is easier to compare the climate in San Francisco and Los Angeles. Try your ideas to see if they work. Use your exercise book.

1 A border problem (PB p. 82/ex. 2)

a) Identify the ***relative clauses*** in the text.
Mark the different types in different colours: ***defining relative clauses*** in red, ***non-defining relative clauses*** in green, ***commenting relative clauses*** in blue. Put brackets round the relative pronouns which can be left out to make ***contact clauses.***

The US has two borders that divide it from its neighbors. The border with Canada, which lies to the north, is 4,000 miles long, which makes it twice the length of the Mexican border. So it might be expected that this is the one (that) the Americans are more likely to have trouble with.

In fact most illegal immigrants, whose aim is to make a better life for themselves in the US, come into the country from the south. It is estimated that each year between 400,000 and a million illegal aliens try to cross the rivers and deserts (which) the border with Mexico runs through. Official statistics, which are given in government reports, show that one in five of these people are caught by the officers whose job is to patrol the border. However, although the officers can be certain about the number of those (who) they arrest, it is impossible for them to be sure about the number that get past them.

One definite trend, which is shown by the nationality of the aliens who are caught, is the increasing number of 'Other than Mexicans', or 'OTMs'. Mexicans, who are traditionally thought of as the main nationality (which) the border officers have to deal with, do still form the majority. However, between 2000 and 2005 the numbers of 'OTMs' (many of them from Honduras and Brazil) rose from 28,598 to 65,814, which is a dramatic increase.

Whether the illegal immigrants are Mexican or 'OTMs', many Americans see a serious problem with their southern border, which has led many of them to call for more and better fences. Some people, who believe that modern technology can help, suggest a 'virtual' fence, which would be constructed of cameras, lights and electronic equipment, and past which nobody at all would be able to slip without being seen.

b) Discuss in groups what your feelings are about the people in the photo.

2 Agriculture in California (PB p. 82/ex. 4) *(Lösung: S. 80)*

Use ***defining*** or ***non-defining relative clauses*** to link the two sentences. (Think about the sense to help you decide which information should go in the relative clause and what other changes you need to make.) Write the new sentences in your exercise book.

1. Agriculture is a leading industry in California. Much of the state's wealth comes from it.
2. Many people work in this part of the economy. They grow fruit and vegetables.
3. California usually has warm and sunny weather. Farmers want this kind of weather.
4. The state produces many wines. Their quality is among the best in the world.
5. Other farmers also make a contribution to the economy. Their products are not crops.
6. The farms provide many jobs for workers. The workers' families need the money.
7. The San Joaquin Valley lies between San Francisco and Los Angeles. It is the largest dairy region in the world.
8. But some people are not happy about the dairy farms. They have to live near the farms.
9. The cows pollute the air. They each produce 19.3 pounds of gases a year.
10. Smog is bad enough in Los Angeles. It is even worse in parts of the San Joaquin Valley!

3 Comments about English (PB p. 82/ex. 4) *(Erwartungshorizont)*

Use a construction with ***which*** to add your own comments to these statements.

1. More people learn English than any other language in the world,
   which *means you can use it to communicate everywhere*.
2. English is the main language on the internet,
   which is a result of the American influence in computer technology.
3. In different English-speaking countries the accent is different,
   which makes it possible to guess where people come from.
4. English spelling can be quite difficult,
   which often causes problems for students.
5. Lots of great pop songs are sung in English,
   which can help to motivate kids to learn the language.
6. Many English words are used in German,
   which not all Germans are happy about!

4 Phrases with prepositions (PB p. 82/ex. 4)

a) Match the phrases below to the prepositions they are followed by.

to be afraid · to apply · to depend · to be good · to have a right · to be interested · to look forward · to be sick · to spend money · to stare · to take part · to wait

	Phrases	Preposition
1	*to be good* / *to stare*	*at*
2	*to apply* / *to wait*	*for*
3	*to be interested* / *to take part*	*in*
4	*to be afraid* / *to be sick*	*of*
5	*to depend* / *to spend money*	*on*
6	*to have a right* / *to look forward*	*to*

b) Choose one phrase from each pair and think of a sentence to show how it is used with the preposition. Write your sentences in your exercise book.
(Erwartungshorizont: S. 80)

⟨5⟩ What's the difference? (PB p. 82/ex. 4)

Use a dictionary to understand these jokes.

1. What's the difference between a cat and a comma?
A cat has claws at the end of its paws, while a comma has a pause at the end of its clause.

2. What's the difference between a fisherman and a bad student?
A fisherman baits his hooks, while a bad student hates his books.

3. What's the difference between a train driver and a teacher?
A train driver minds the train, while a teacher trains the mind.

1 Julia's memories (PB p. 84/ex. 2)

Complete what Julia says about her time in the tree.
Find your own verbs, using ***participles*** for longer actions and ***infinitives*** for shorter ones.

"It was always a special moment when I saw the sun *begin/start* to rise in the morning. It was wonderful to watch the light *spreading* over the sky and to listen to the birds *singing* to greet the new day. And it was fascinating to see the forest *changing* gradually from one season to another. I was also always happy to see my friends *arrive/standing* at the bottom of the tree and to hear them *shout/call* hello. Every day they put food in a basket for me, and when I saw them *give* the signal, I pulled the basket up on a rope. Of course not everything was great. During storms it was scary to feel the tree *moving/shaking* in the terrible wind and rain, and I was also scared when I saw the helicopter *coming/flying* down to harass me. For a number of nights I was forced to listen to the timber crews *making* a noise so I couldn't sleep. I felt myself *getting/becoming* angry, but in the end I managed to stay calm. It was a fantastic moment when I heard the manager of the timber company *promise* not to cut Luna down. When I felt my feet *touch* the ground again at last after two years, I was so happy that I cried!"

2 Famous people (PB p. 84/ex. 2)

a) Some kids are boasting about famous people they have seen. Complete what they say with ***verbs of perception*** and ***participles*** or ***infinitives***. *(Erwartungshorizont: S. 80)*

1. I saw Julia Hill yesterday! I noticed her …
2. That's nothing! I've seen Robbie Williams. I …
3. Well, I've seen Madonna! I …
4. I was in the same restaurant as Elton John! I …
5. A few weeks ago I spotted Jennifer Lopez. I …
6. I bet none of you have seen Tom Cruise! I …

b) In groups, boast about the famous people you have seen. (It needn't be true!)
Use ***verbs of perception*** with ***participles*** or ***infinitives*** to express their actions.

3 Word building: Nouns (PB p. 84/ex. 2)

a) Find the correct endings to make nouns from the verbs. If necessary, use a dictionary.

achieve • annoy • apologise • appear • begin • create • develop • discover • enjoy • injure • meet • perform • pollute • protect • refuse • remove • survive • understand

1 (-ion)	2 (-ment)	3 (-ing)
creation	*achievement*	*beginning*
pollution	*development*	*meeting*
protection	*enjoyment*	*understanding*

4 (-ance)	5 (-al)	6 (-y)
annoyance	*refusal*	*apology*
appearance	*removal*	*discovery*
performance	*survival*	*injury*

b) Rewrite these sentences using nouns in place of the **marked** verbs. (You may also need to make other changes to the sentences.) Use your exercise book. *(Erwartungshorizont: S. 80)*

1. Last year I went on a trip to learn how to **survive** in the wilderness.
2. Every night I had to make a shelter to **protect** myself against the weather.
3. One day I was given a shock when a big bear **appeared** in front of me.
4. Another day I slipped on some rocks, but luckily the fall didn't **injure** me.
5. I'm proud of what I **achieved** and I also feel I **understand** nature much better now.

c) Choose one more noun from each box in **a)** and write your own sentences in your exercise book. *(Erwartungshorizont: S. 80)*

4 Everyday English: Expressions with *and* (PB p. 84/ex. 2)

a) Some expressions often used in English are a pair of words, with either a similar or an opposite meaning, that are linked by ***and***. Complete the sentences with pairs of words from **A** and **B**.
Example: We stood and talked about this and that.

A here • clean • sick • now • ~~this~~ • high • peace

B tired • ~~that~~ • low • quiet • then • tidy • there

1. It's great to get away from the city and enjoy the *peace* and *quiet* of nature.
2. Please don't make a mess, kids! Keep the tent *clean* and *tidy*.
3. Apparently there are picnic tables *here* and *there* in the forest.
4. It's a very hot day, so *now* and *then* we'll need to stop and have a drink.
5. I've looked *high* and *low*, but I can't find the sunscreen anywhere.
6. I'm *sick* and *tired* of looking at big trees. I want to do something different.

b) Discuss with a partner how you can best translate the expressions in **a)** into German. Use a dictionary to check your translations. *(Erwartungshorizont: S. 80)*

5 Mediation: Questions and answers (PB p. 84/ex. 3) *(Erwartungshorizont)*

Julia Hill is taking part in a talk show in Germany. She doesn't speak German, so you are interpreting. Put the questions into English for her and then give her answers in German.

1. *Question:* Hast du damals alleine gehandelt, um den Baum zu retten?

   You: *Did you act alone to save the tree?*
   Julia: No, I was just one of many activists trying to save the forest.

   You: *Nein, ich war nur eine von vielen Aktivistinnen und Aktivisten, die versuchten, den Wald zu retten*

2. *Question:* Woher habt ihr gewusst, dass eine Holzfirma den Baum fällen wollte?

   You: *How did you know that a timber company wanted to cut down the tree?*
   Julia: We'd heard cutting somewhere on the hill, so we went to find out what was going on.

   You: *Wir hörten, wie irgendwo auf dem Hügel gesägt wurde. Deshalb gingen wir hin, um herauszufinden, was los war.*

3. *Question:* Du hast ganz hoch oben im Baum gelebt, oder? Wie bist du da hingekommen?

   You: *You lived high up in the tree, didn't you? How did you get up there?*
   Julia: We used rock-climbing gear, also to pull up stuff to build a platform and shelter.

   You: *Wir benutzten eine Kletterausrüstung, auch um das Zeug zum Bauen einer Plattform und Schutzhütte hochzuziehen.*

4. *Question:* Hat keiner versucht, euch davon abzuhalten?

   You: *Didn't anybody try to stop you?*
   Julia: No, we did it all at night by moonlight. That's where Luna got her name!

   You: *Nein, wir machten das alles nachts bei Mondschein. So erhielt Luna ihren Namen!*

5. *Question:* Und dein Name? Warum nennt man dich 'Butterfly'?

   You: *And what about your name? Why are you called/do people call you 'Butterfly'?*
   Julia: Because once, while I was out hiking, a butterfly followed me all day long!

   You: *Weil mir einmal beim Wandern den ganzen Tag lang ein Schmetterling folgte.*

6 Mediation: Information for visitors (PB p. 84/ex. 3) *(Erwartungshorizont: S. 80)*

A lot of people from other countries visit America's national parks, so visitors' centres provide important information in different languages. Translate the text on the right for a brochure in German about wildlife in Yosemite.

Don't be *bear* careless!

Each year black bears are killed in Yosemite as a direct result of human carelessness. We call it a bear problem, but bears are not to blame.

Driven by their powerful sense of smell, black bears are drawn to human food. Once bears get this food, they continue to seek it out – from backpacks, picnic tables and even visitors' cars. Their natural fear of people fades and they may become aggressive. When they become too aggressive, they often have to be killed. The only way to stop this is to make sure that all food items are stored properly.

1 An internet report (PB p. 87/ex. 3)

a) Read the text. Using techniques you have learnt, guess the meaning of the following words. Write down the German translation for them, then check with a dictionary to see if you are correct.

1. destruction (line 5): *Zerstörung*
2. priests (line 6): *Priester/Geistliche*
3. walks of life (line 7): *alle Schichten und Berufe*
4. tissue products (line 8): *Papierprodukte*
5. toilet bowls (line 9): *Kloschüsseln*
6. pedestrian areas (line 11): *Fußgängerzonen*
7. awareness (line 12): *Bewusstsein*
8. market researchers (line 14): *Marktforscher*
9. colleagues (line 18): *Kollegen*

Day of action against Kimberly Clark

campaigns
reports
contact

Kimberly Clark is flushing old-growth trees down the toilet, and on November 3, activists across the country took action to stop it. More than 350 demonstrations in cities and towns across the continent proved just how serious consumers are about stopping the destruction of ancient forests.

From college students to moms, veterans to priests, people from all walks of life joined together to demand that Kimberly Clark use recycled paper in its disposable tissue products. In San Francisco, we set up 30 toilet bowls in a public square, to demonstrate how consumers are flushing away ancient forests. Activists placed models of clearcuts in busy pedestrian areas and organized information tables at schools and universities – all to raise awareness and to pressure Kimberly Clark to stop wiping away ancient forests. And that's not all!

- In California, high school student Rohini and other activists dressed up as market researchers in white coats and glasses to challenge people to tell the difference between Kleenex and forest-friendly toilet paper.
- In Williamsburg, Virginia, Cheryl took part in the day of action during her lunch hour with colleagues, visiting the local store to discuss alternative products with the manager.

Thousands of other activists are calling and sending letters to Kimberly Clark. It's not too late to join in – you can call Kimberly Clark today and say what you think about flushing old-growth trees down the toilet.

b) Use your dictionary again to look up 'wipe (away)'. Then explain the two meanings in the phrase 'stop wiping away ancient forests' (line 13). Write your answer in your exercise book. *(Erwartungshorizont: S. 80)*

c) Role play: With a partner, act the scene from the day of action in which Cheryl visits her local store manager. Cheryl explains the issue and tries to persuade the manager to sell only forest-friendly products. The manager can decide whether to give a positive or negative reaction to what Cheryl says.

d) Imagine you want to support the day of action. Write a letter to Kimberly Clark. When you have finished, check your letter and think how you can improve what you have written. The tips on pages 66–67 in your book can help you.

⟨**e)**⟩ In groups, choose another environmental issue you think is important. Think of ways to raise public awareness. Make a plan for a day of action.

2 Listening: A Californian from Austria[1] (PB p. 87/ex. 3) *(Erwartungshorizont)*

a) Listen for dates in the conversation. Note them down and also the information given about that year. (You will probably need to listen a few times.)

Date	Information
1947	*born in Austria/Graz*
1962	*started bodybuilding*
1967	*became Mr Universe (for first time)*
1968	*moved to the US*
1979	*got business qualification*
1984	*'Terminator'; became US citizen*
1986	*got married (to Maria Shriver)*
1997	*heart problems*
2003	*became Governor of California*

b) Imagine you have the chance to interview Arnold Schwarzenegger. Think of six questions you would like to ask him and write them in your exercise book.
(Erwartungshorizont: S. 80)

[1] ['ɒstriə] – Österreich

3 Debating politely (PB p. 88) *(Erwartungshorizont)*

In a debate it is important to respect other people and their point of view. Help these people to express themselves more politely or in a more correct style.

1. "Only an idiot could possibly think what you've just said!"

   "I'm afraid I don't share your opinion/disagree with you strongly."

2. "Hey! Stop interrupting other people all the time."

   "I really must ask you not to interrupt."

3. "You're not wrong there, mate!"

   "I absolutely agree with what you say."

4. "You obviously weren't listening to what I was saying."

   "Perhaps I didn't express myself clearly enough."

5. "Come on, guys! You know I'm right, don't you?"

   "I hope I've managed to persuade you."

6. "Hands up if you think the statement is right."

   "May I please have your votes for the statement."

1 Columbia (PB p. 89/ex. 2)

Use the ideas to make sentences with different kinds of ***relative clauses***. (Sometimes there is more than one way to link the information.)

1. Columbia • lies east of San Francisco • once important town

   Columbia, which lies east of San Francisco, was once an important town.

2. gold found here in 1850 • started a gold rush

   The gold which was found here in 1850 started a gold rush.

3. today visitors • go to Columbia • travel back in time

   Today visitors who go to Columbia travel back in time.

4. role players • their costumes are from the 1850s • act out everyday life

   Role players, whose costumes are from the 1850s, act out everyday life.

5. many events • visitors can take part in them

   There are many events in which visitors can take part.

6. all kinds of attractions • makes it a great place to visit

   There are all kinds of attractions, which makes it a great place to visit.

2 Cloze test: From a travel diary (PB p. 89/ex. 3)

Every seventh word in the text is missing. Read the whole text first, then go back and complete it.

Yesterday evening I met a girl *who* offered to give me a surfing *lesson*. As she said, it would be *a* pity for a guy from England *to* come over here to California and *not* to learn how to ride the *waves*. So this morning my new friend, *whose* name is Kristi, took me to *her* favourite surfing beach and tried to *teach* me a few basic skills. But *I* was a hopeless student. Poor Kristi *had* to spend all morning watching me *fall* over whenever I tried to stand *up*. I must have looked really funny *because* in the end she started to *laugh*. I could see some other kids *watching* and laughing, too. When Kristi finally *gave* up with my lesson, they invited *us* both to the barbecue they were *having* on the beach. I can't believe *how* friendly the kids here are. Almost *everyone/body* in California is so laidback. I *think* their attitude is great. I may *be* really bad at surfing but I *could* easily get used to life here.

Tandem Activity 3

A

Plan a weekend in Los Angeles with your partner. You each have different extracts from a guide book. Study your extracts. Use a dictionary to look up any new words and be prepared to explain them to your partner. Then make suggestions for sightseeing. Give reasons for your suggestions and comment on your partner's ideas. Discuss all the different possibilities, express your likes and dislikes and make your plan. Follow these rules:

– You can visit a total of no more than five places.
– Together you must spend no more than $135.

Various companies offer tours of **Beverly Hills,** giving you the opportunity to look at the homes of famous stars (only the outside, mind!). A two-hour trip by Starline Tours costs $32.

Formed in 1924 the **Hollywood Reservoir** provided the drinking water which enabled the city to grow. Now most of its water storage is underground, but the pretty lake has trails around it which offer a fantastic view of the Hollywood sign.

Los Angeles County Museum of Art houses a large collection that covers everything from modern American art to ancient Islamic works. Open daily noon–8pm; admission $9; under-17s free.

Disneyland is packed with exciting adventure rides and attractions. From the Space Mountain rollercoaster to Mickey Mouse in Fantasyland, there's so much to do that you won't know where to begin.
All-day ticket $47; under-3s free.

It's definitely worth walking around **Little Tokyo** and enjoying the atmosphere. Across from Japanese Village Plaza, a mall with restaurants, shops and karaoke bars, you'll find a wonderful romantic example of a traditional Japanese garden.

B

Plan a weekend in Los Angeles with your partner. You each have different extracts from a guide book. Study your extracts. Use a dictionary to look up any new words and be prepared to explain them to your partner. Then make suggestions for sightseeing. Give reasons for your suggestions and comment on your partner's ideas. Discuss all the different possibilities, express your likes and dislikes and make your plan. Follow these rules:

– You can visit a total of no more than five places.
– Together you must spend no more than $135.

People-watching is the main activity at **Venice Beach**. Join in with the joggers and skaters on the boardwalk, or watch the bodybuilders working out.

A visit to **Universal Studios** gives you the chance to see behind the scenes at a working Hollywood studio and also to meet many of your favorite movie characters. It's one of the most popular attractions in LA, though, so be prepared for crowds.
Admission $49; under-3s free.

The spectacular **Aquarium of the Pacific** has been open since 1998. Lovable sea lions, colorful fish, and scary sharks – a lot of Pacific ocean life is there to be seen.
Open 9am–6pm daily; admission $18.95.

In the courtyard of **Grauman's Chinese Theater** around 200 stars have made their hand and/or footprints in wet cement. For $9 you can measure your own hands and feet against the likes of Tom Cruise and Britney Spears!

The theme of the **Museum of the American West** is the history and culture of the various population groups of the American west.
Open 10am–5pm Tue, Wed, Fri–Sun; 10am–8pm Thur; admission $7.50.

Focus on literature

15 1 Listening: Interview with a young writer (PB p. 90/ex. 1)

a) Kate Massey is being interviewed about her first novel[1]. Listen and fill in the grid.

Kate's age	*16*	Title of novel	*'Full moon'*
Her reaction to winning a prize	*amazed; could hardly believe it*		
Setting of the novel	*New York; present and future*		
Central character(s)	*Sam; terrible bully*		
Narrator	*Sam*	Points of view	*Sam as a boy and as a ninety-year-old man*
E-mail address of radio programme	*booklovers@youthradio.uk*		

b) Make notes on these points in your exercise book. Listen again if you need to. *(Erwartungshorizont: S. 80)*

1. The plot of Kate's novel.
2. How the novel got its title.
3. Where Kate got the idea for her book.
4. The image Kate uses to describe the process of writing her book.
5. Kate's four tips for young writers.
6. Kate's feelings about her success – what she likes and doesn't like.

[1]['nɒvl] – Roman

c) What would you like to ask Kate? Write an e-mail with two or three questions.

2 A bestseller (PB p. 90/ex. 3)

a) How do you think the author felt about these reviews? Explain why in your exercise book. *(Erwartungshorizont: S. 80)*

b) Work in groups to collect adjectives and phrases you might expect to find in reviews of bestsellers and list them in your exercise book. Use your dictionary, if necessary. (Don't forget that some bestsellers get bad reviews!)

"I have never read anything quite like Mark Haddon's funny and honest book ... I advise you to buy two copies; you won't want to lend yours out." Arthur Golden

"OUTSTANDING ... A stunningly good read!" INDEPENDENT

"A brilliant and heart-warming book." SCOTSMAN

"A superb achievement." Ian McEwan

"A funny as well as a sad book ... brilliant." GUARDIAN

"Not simply the most original novel I've read in years ... it's also one of the best." THE TIMES

"The oddest and most original narrator to appear in years." INDEPENDENT

"It's beautifully written ... I couldn't wait to turn each page." Anne Tyler

"Mark Haddon shows great understanding of the autistic[3] mind ... I found it all very moving, very believable and very funny." Oliver Sacks

[2]['kjʊəriəs ˌɪntsɪdnt] – merkwürdiger Vorfall • [3][ɔː'tɪstɪk] – autistisch *(krankhaft ichbezogen und teilnahmslos gegenüber der Umwelt)*

c) Complete this review of Mark Haddon's book. Put in the numbers of the missing words.

1 **tell**	5 **parent**	9 **out**	13 **narrator**	17 **events**
2 **adult**	6 **on**	10 **published**	14 **author**	18 **resistance**
3 **plot**	7 **setting**	11 **perspective**	15 **brown**	19 **world**
4 **character**	8 **unusual**	12 ~~**mystery**~~	16 **story**	20 **him**

This strange murder [12] novel took the public by storm when it was first [10] in 2003. The story is told from the [11] of a teenager, but was written by an [2], the [14] Mark Haddon. The central [4] and [13] is Christopher Boone, who is fifteen years old and suffers from a mild form of autism. In his world, red things are good but yellow and [15] things are bad, and people should never [1] lies. Christopher loves facts and lists. He hates being touched.

The [7] is the English town of Swindon, where Christopher lives with his father, a single [5]. The [17] begin on the opening page. Christopher, who has never gone further than the end of the road [6] his own, decides to find [9] who killed his neighbour's dog with a garden fork. As the [3] develops, we meet his father, his teacher, his pet rat, his neighbours, and the [8] facts he keeps locked away in his brain. Christopher faces [18] from adults as he tries to investigate the dog's death, which – by chance – leads [20] to begin investigating the story of his dead mother. The beauty of the book isn't the detective [16], but the unusual understanding of the mind of a boy living in a [19] with different rules to his own.

d) Read this chapter from the novel and then answer the questions on page 71. Use your exercise book.
(Erwartungshorizont: S. 81)

This is a murder mystery novel.

Siobhan said that I should write something I would want to read myself. Mostly I read books about science and maths. I do not like proper novels. In proper novels people say things like, "I am veined with iron, with silver and with streaks of common mud." What does this mean? I do not know. Nor does Father. Nor do Siobhan or Mr Jeavons. I have asked them.

Siobhan has long blonde hair and wears glasses which are made of green plastic. And Mr Jeavons smells of soap and wears brown shoes that have approximately 60 tiny circular holes in each of them.

But I do like murder mystery novels. So I am writing a murder mystery novel. In a murder mystery novel someone has to work out who the murderer is and then catch them. It is a puzzle. If it is a good puzzle you can sometimes work out the answer before the end of the book.

Siobhan said that this book should begin with something to grab people's attention. That is why I started with the dog. I also started with the dog because it happened to me and I find it hard to imagine things which did not happen to me.

Siobhan read the first page and said that it was different. She put this word into inverted commas by making the wiggly quotation sign with her first and second fingers. She said it was usually people who were killed in murder mystery novels. I said that two dogs were killed in 'The Hound[1] of the Baskervilles', the hound itself and James Mortimer's spaniel, but Siobhan said that they weren't the victims[2] of the murder, Sir Charles Baskerville was. She said that this was because readers cared more about people than dogs, so if a person was killed in the book readers would want to carry on reading.

I said that I wanted to write about something real and I knew people who had died but I did not know any people who had been killed, except Edward's father from school, Mr Paulson, and that it was a gliding accident, not murder, and I didn't really know him. I also said that I cared about dogs because they were faithful and honest, and some dogs were cleverer and more interesting than people. Steve, for example, who comes to school on Thursdays, needs help to eat his food and could not even fetch a stick. Siobhan asked me not to say this to Steve's mother.

From: The curious incident of the dog in the night-time

Mark Haddon

[1][haʊnd] – Jagdhund • [2][ˈvɪktɪmz] – Opfer

1. Who is the narrator and the main character of this novel?
2. What do you think Christopher means by 'proper' novels?
3. Give examples of the kind of books Christopher enjoys. Why does he prefer them to 'proper' novels?
4. Compare your taste in books with Christopher's. What is the same, and what is different?
5. What do we learn about Christopher that shows he suffers from autism? Give examples.
6. What two tips does Siobhan give him for writing his novel? What is your opinion of her tips?
7. Describe the style of writing and the effect it has on the reader. Say whether you think the style is typical of a murder mystery novel, and explain why.

3 Interpreting a poem (PB p. 93/ex. 4) *(Erwartungshorizont: S. 81)*

Dreams

Hold fast to dreams
For if dreams die
Life is a broken-winged bird
That cannot fly

Hold fast to dreams
For when dreams go
Life is a barren field
Frozen with snow

Langston Hughes

Langston Hughes (1902–1967) is one of the most famous black poets of the 20th century.

a) Look up any new words and read the poem aloud. Then think about the images that are used in the poem and explain what they might mean.

b) Now try to interpret the poem. Explain the message without using any of the poem's imagery. Also think about the use of rhyme and repetitions.

⟨c)⟩ Creative writing: Think about what else should be 'held fast' and write your own poem.

4 Project: 'Books you must read before you grow up' (PB p. 93/ex. 4)

a) Your class is going to create a collection of book reviews, called 'Books you must read before you grow up'. First brainstorm together how many books to include, and which ones. You may include novels, plays, short stories and poetry. The books need not be examples of English literature, but the reviews must be written in English and no more than 300 words.

b) Work in groups to write the reviews. If each person writes a different review, discuss the book first in your group to get ideas for what to write. Check your reviews for mistakes before you put your collection together.

Useful phrases …

- This is a novel/play/short story/poem about …
- It was published in …
- The author is …
- The narrator is …
- The main character is …
- It is told from the perspective of …
- It deals with/It is about …
- It is set in/It takes place in/The setting is …
- The story is based on real/fictional[1] events.
- It reaches a climax/the turning point when …
- It gives the reader an insight into …
- The book won the … prize for literature in …
- The book has a happy/sad ending.
- I advise you to read the book because …

[1] ['fɪkʃnl] – erfunden

Test practice 1

16 1 Listening: Our throw-away society (PB p. 95/ex. 3)

a) Listen to part of a radio interview with Tom Nicholson, a council[1] officer from Lichfield, England, and Diana Jolly, from Friends of the Earth. Look at the text before listening again. Then complete the sentences.

1. According to statistics, every person in *Britain* throws away *half* a ton of rubbish a *year*. If waste from *industry*, construction work and so on is included, the total amount comes to over 400 *million* tons. 'Landfill sites' are conveniently *cheap* places to put our *rubbish*, but even modern landfill sites still give off harmful *gases* that are bad for the *environment*. In Britain, less than *twenty* percent of *household* waste is recycled or turned into compost, although in theory it could be about *seventy* percent!

2. A lot of the rubbish *collected* for recycling is sent *abroad* to developing *countries*. Another way of *dealing* with the problem is to *burn* the waste in the UK, but this method is not safe with *plastic*, metal or glass. *Mobile* phones are a problem because so many of them are *thrown* away and they are full of *dangerous* chemicals and *metals*. Although old phones and other *electronic* equipment can be given back to the manufacturers, this hasn't solved the *problem* yet.

[1]['kaʊntsl] – Stadtrat

b) How can you – as an individual – help to reduce the amount of household waste? Write about 100 words in your exercise book. *(Erwartungshorizont: S. 81)*

2 C-test: Not as green as they look (PB p. 95/ex. 3)

Complete the text. Each blank (_) stands for one letter.

Putting a wind turbine[2] on your roof to help the environment sounds like a good idea. But i*t* isn't wo*rth* it. Gr*een* campaigners wa*rn* that turb*ines* on t*he* roof d*o* little t*o* reduce green*house* gases. Th*ey* may an*noy* your neigh*bours*, and ca*use* vibrations th*at* could dam*age* your ho*me*, and wi*ll* only pro*duce* enough elect*ricity* to po*wer* a hairdryer! Fri*ends* of t*he* Earth adv*ise* people aga*inst* investing i*n* these fashi*onable* 'windmills[3]'. Instead they suggest a number of efficient ways of saving energy in the home.

[2]['wɪnd ˌtɜːbaɪn] – Windturbine • [3]['wɪndmɪlz] – Windmühlen

3 Mediation: Melting glaciers in the Alps (PB p. 95/ex. 3) *(Erwartungshorizont: S. 81)*

A British friend who is staying with you in Bavaria wants you to explain what this article is about. First mark the most important points in the text. Then give the main facts in English.
Use your exercise book. These words will be useful: degree [dɪ'griː] – Grad;
glacier ['glæsiə] – Gletscher; to melt [melt] – schmelzen; temperature ['temprətʃə]

Klimawandel: Die Erwärmung verändert besonders die Bergwelt

Klimaforscher befürchten, dass bis 2050 drei Viertel der Gletscher in Mitteleuropa verschwunden sein werden.

Seit Beginn der modernen Gletscherforschung um 1860 haben die alpinen Eisfelder bis 1970 im Durchschnitt ein Drittel ihrer Fläche und die Hälfte ihres Volumens verloren. Wissenschaftler und Umweltschützer beunruhigt vor allem die rasant zunehmende Geschwindigkeit des Rückzugs: Die 5.150 Alpengletscher, die es im Jahr 1970 noch gab, haben seither weitere 40 Prozent ihrer Masse eingebüßt – allein im Hitzesommer 2003 gingen 5 bis 10 Prozent den Bach runter.

Seit 1900 ist die globale Durchschnittstemperatur um circa 0,8 Grad gestiegen, an der Nordseite der Alpen aber um 1,8 Grad. Die Schneefallgrenze ist gut 150 Meter bergaufwärts gewandert. Falls die Durchschnittstemperatur in den Alpen bis 2100 um weitere 3 Grad zulegt, wie Studien eines UNO-Gremiums erwarten, könnte sich nur ein kümmerlicher Bruchteil der Gletscher von 1850 halten. Bei einem Anstieg um 5 Grad würden die Alpen praktisch eisfrei.

Die Umweltverbände haben keinen Zweifel daran, dass die Erwärmung vom Menschen verursacht wird. Aber selbst wenn alle auf Fahrrad und Bahn umsteigen, Ökostrom abonnieren, Wegwerfprodukte meiden und Briefe an Politiker schreiben würden, wären die Gletscher kaum noch zu retten.

Sind wir womöglich die letzte Generation, die in den Alpen Gletscher erleben kann? Schnell noch die glänzenden Wahrzeichen der Alpen anschauen, bevor sie ganz weggetaut sind!

4 Population growth in the US (PB p. 95/ex. 3)

There are twelve words missing from this text. They are below – but not in the right order.
Find the right place for each word and write it in. Use each word only once.

Over the hundred years, the number people living in the US has been rising steadily. The population
past *of*
hit 100 million 1915, and 200 million in 1967. In 2006 it 300 million, but few were celebrating.
in *reached*
Americans today have begun to feel about growth. Far from it as a good sign, most now associate it
different *seeing*
with sprawl, increase of traffic and environmental damage. In many ways this is true. During the last
urban
40 years or so, much of the country has been into suburban areas, and every day open space is lost to
turned
more and stores. On the hand, the US remains a huge, largely empty country. Compared with Europe,
houses *other*
which serious problems as its population figures fall, America is fortunate. Maybe its population
faces
growth should be after all.
celebrated

celebrated | different | faces | houses | in | of | other | ~~past~~ | reached | seeing | turned | urban

1 Listening: Problems (PB p. 97/ex. 5) *(Erwartungshorizont: S. 81)*

Wendy Cooper and Bill Johnson work for the Problem Page of a magazine. Each week they work through the letters they receive and decide which ones to put in the magazine. This morning Bill has not been in the office. Now he is talking to Wendy in the lunch break. Listen to their conversation. Then look at the exercises before listening again.

a) Explain each person's problem in a few sentences. Write in your exercise book.

b) Choose one of the problems you have heard about, and write a reply from Wendy or Bill (60–100 words). Use your exercise book.

2 Reading comprehension: The date[1] (PB p. 97/ex. 5) *(Erwartungshorizont: S. 81)*

a) Read the cartoon and compare it to the text below. Then underline any mistakes that you can find in the text and correct them in your exercise book.

Paige wants to go to the cinema with her friend Nicole tomorrow, and asks Nicole's brother Peter if he'd like to go with them. But Peter's going out with Susie tomorrow. Although Paige likes Susie, Peter can't stand her, so Paige wonders why he's got this date with her. Peter explains that Susie had brought some fireworks to school, and when she showed them to him in their History lesson, he suddenly felt attracted to her. But Paige thinks Peter's feelings towards Susie only changed because she had tickets for a fantastic concert.

While they're sitting in the taxi on the way to the concert, Susie thanks Peter for buying her the tickets. She admits how amazed she was to be invited to the concert, because she thought Peter didn't like her at all. But Peter is honest with her, telling her he's got nothing against her. Then Susie says she could easily understand Peter for hating her, because of all the boring things she keeps doing. In the end, she admits she forgot to buy the tickets.

b) Now write the answers to these questions in your exercise book.

1. Why do you think Paige calls Peter her 'favorite' brother?
2. Describe how Peter's feelings towards Susie change (twice!), and explain why.
3. Would you go out with someone you didn't like if they had tickets for a concert you wanted to go to? Explain why.

[1] [deɪt] – Verabredung

3 Error spotting: Interested in modelling (PB p. 97/ex. 5)

Decide whether the underlined words and phrases are correct or not. Use the lines on the right to correct any mistakes you find. If there is no mistake, write in the word 'correct'.

I have a <u>16-years-old</u> **(1)** English cousin, and lots	1. *16-year-old*
of friends of <u>her</u> **(2)** and other people she knows,	2. *hers*
including a professional photographer, <u>have told</u> **(3)**	3. *correct*
her that she could be <u>a model</u> **(4)**. She wrote to an	4. *correct*
<u>adress</u> **(5)** she saw in a magazine and soon they sent	5. *address*
<u>to her</u> **(6)** a list of good modelling agents. However,	6. *her*
she was <u>disappointing</u> **(7)** to see that all the best ones	7. *disappointed*
were in London (and she lives <u>nearby</u> **(8)** the Welsh	8. *near*
border, <u>what</u> **(9)** would mean a very long journey).	9. *which*
So if she wanted to do modelling, she <u>had to</u> **(10)**	10. *would have to*
travel <u>every time to London</u> **(11)**. All in all, she's	11. *to London every time*
decided <u>it's</u> **(12)** not worth it.	12. *correct*

4 Cloze test: New centres to help homeless teens (PB p. 97/ex. 5)

Complete the text with suitable words. (Every seventh word is missing.)

Children who are kicked out of *their* homes by their own parents after *having* rows with them will soon be *able* to stay in a nationwide network *of* 'cooling off centres' which are planned *as* part of a government campaign to *beat/fight/prevent* youth homelessness. The few centres of *this* kind that already exist in England *have* been highly praised, and ministers intend *to* establish one in at least 340 *British/different* towns. Each year 20,000 young people *become* homeless in this way. Rows with *parents/families* are the most common contributor to *the* total of 80,000 people who end *up* without a home every year.

Weitere Lösungen und Erwartungshorizonte *(EH)*

S. 4 **4a)** *(EH)* 2. While they were surfing, a message in a bottle arrived on a big wave. 3. She was reading a comic/magazine when one of the legs on her chair broke and the chair fell over. 4. He was lying in the bath when a bird suddenly flew in through the open window. 5. While they were collecting money for a charity, someone gave them free ice creams. 6. While she was waiting for a bus, a TV star walked past. 7. They were playing football when a helicopter suddenly landed near them.

S. 5 **1)** *(EH) A*: Girls are usually crazy about following the latest fashions. *B*: Hey, not only girls! Lots of boys enjoy wearing nice clothes, too. *A*: Young people are generally interested in learning about new technology. *B*: That's true. I mean, most kids are good at using computers. *A*: Lots of kids dream of becoming pop stars. *B*: Yes, they imagine singing in front of thousands of fans. *A*: Teenagers don't usually feel like doing homework. *B*: I know, but at the same time most of them are worried about getting bad grades, so they do their homework anyway! **3b)** I'll never forget tasting Indian food for the first time. I'd stopped to try it at an Asian street festival. I remember thinking how delicious it was. Since then eating Indian food has meant going to a restaurant. But now I mean to learn to cook it myself. I'm trying to find a course that teaches authentic recipes. I won't forget to invite you for a meal. Stop looking so worried – I'll practise first!

S. 7 **7)** *(EH)* **A.** Japans neuester, superschneller Zug wurde zum ersten Mal vorgestellt. Er hat Ohren wie die einer Katze! Der Fastech 360S fährt 360 Stundenkilometer und die Ohren auf dem Dach helfen, den Zug im Notfall anzuhalten. Ab 2011 wird der Zug voraussichtlich in Betrieb sein. **B.** In Taiwan wurde ein neues Restaurant eröffnet, in dem man beim Essen auf Stühlen sitzt, die die Form einer Toilette haben! Andere außergewöhnliche Restaurants sind zum Beispiel das ‚taube' Restaurant in Paris, in dem man das Essen in Zeichensprache bestellt sowie das ‚blinde' Restaurant in London, in dem man im Dunkeln isst. **8a)** *(EH)* You can translate the first joke because it depends on the situation that is described, so the language isn't important. You can't translate the second joke into German because the word 'last' has two meanings in English, but in German you have to use two different words.

S. 8 **1b)** *(EH)* 1. ... a lot of them drink too much. 2. they want to show that they can do what they like. 3. ... is trying to teach children in schools about the danger to their health. 4. ... can also be found in other countries in southern Europe. 5. ... advertisements which are aimed at young people by the drinks industry. 6. ... people from different countries often meet and influence each other.

S. 9 **2b)** *(EH)* 4. Older people often do not have access to the internet. 5. Last year the number of street crimes increased (by almost seven percent). 9. Fashion shows are taking place in London this week./American fashion shows took place last month. **2c)** *(EH)* 1. Governments from across the world have already promised help. 2. The money is needed for tents, food and medicines. 3. The reason is that now lots of people use the telephone or the internet. 4. They say banks should protect jobs at home instead of using cheaper workers in countries like India. 5. They are not reported because the chance of getting the objects back is so small. 6. They have been discussing how to reduce damage to the environment without any negative effect on the world economy. 7. They are angry about how much the meetings cost. 8. The clothes all look informal.

S. 10 **1b)** *(EH)* information the text does not give: where the name Sony comes from; who owns the company now; how many countries Sony has factories in; what Sony's profits are; how many PlayStations have been sold; what plans for the future are. **2** 1. Sony started 2. has been the first 3. needed to sell products worldwide 4. became a global company 5. was a huge success 6. had invented a new product **3** *(EH)* 1946: company starts in Tokyo; 1954: success begins with first transistor radio; 1960: forms Sony Corporation of America; 1968: founds Sony UK Limited; invents first colour television; 1972: opens factory in US/San Diego; 1974: opens factory in UK/Bridgend; 1975: world's first home video system; 1979: Walkman; 1981: electronic camera; 1982: world's first CD player; 1983: first consumer camcorder; 1988: forms Sony Music Entertainment; 1989: forms Sony Pictures Entertainment; 1995: PlayStation games machine (huge success).

S. 11 **1b)** *(EH)* 1. Sponsorship is a system that pays sports stars for advertising a company's products. 2. A skateboarder is someone who rides a skateboard. 3. Feedback is information about people's reactions to something. 4. You hold a handrail to prevent yourself from falling down steps or stairs. 5. A deadline is the date or time when something must be completed. 6. Sportswear is the name for the special clothes that are worn for sports. 7. The extra hours that people work after their normal hours is called overtime. 8. Highway is the American word for a main road.

S. 12 **Tandem Activity 1** *(EH)* **Harry's decision** When Harry saw the mp3 player in the shop window, he knew that he had to have it. It looked so cool, and he would also be able to download all his favourite music onto it. Unfortunately it was expensive, and Harry did not have the money to buy it. Then he had an idea. He started to do jobs in the neighbourhood. He washed cars and took dogs for walks, and he saved all the money he was paid. At last, when he counted his money one evening, he found that he had enough. He was very happy and couldn't wait to go back to the shop and buy the mp3 player. However, that same evening Harry saw a programme on TV about children who were starving in Africa. Suddenly the mp3 player did not seem so important any more. The next day Harry walked straight past the shop with the mp3 players and went into a bank where he gave his money to 'Action for Africa'.

S. 14 **2a)** *(EH)* **18th and 19th centuries:** dirty work; work from 7 am to 6 pm; badly paid; lived in poverty; most workers no education/could not read or write; Mary Barrett didn't wear stockings, shoes or trousers; some men were naked; plenty of work for miners. **21st century:** fresh air; machines do a lot of the work; work about eight hours a day; quite good income; miners have good education and receive special training courses; miners wear hard hats, strong boots and special clothing; many mines have closed; difficult for miners to find work. **2b)** *(EH)* In the 18th and 19th centuries a miner's work was dirty and dangerous, but now in the 21st century mines are much safer. There are many machines to do the work which miners had to do themselves before. Fresh air moves around the mines and gets rid of dangerous gases. This helps to make the mine a less dusty place. Before, the miners had to work from 7 am to 6 pm, were badly paid and lived in poverty. In this century, a miner works about eight hours a day and has quite a good income. Miners today have had a school education and many have done special training courses. In Mary Barrett's time, hardly any worker had been to school and very few of them could read or write. When Mary Barrett worked in the mines she didn't wear stockings, shoes or trousers and some of the men were naked. Now miners wear hard hats, strong boots and special clothing to protect themselves. But today many mines have closed in the UK and it is difficult for miners to find work. During the Industrial Revolution there was plenty of work for miners, so it was easy for them to find a job. **3a)** *(EH)* 1. I would not like to have a robot like Aibo because it is much too expensive and I prefer to play with my friends, not a machine or a computer. If I had a dog, I would like a real dog that has feelings and is warm and alive. 2. In my opinion Aibo is not a useful invention. The robot is not a productive machine and doesn't actually make anyone's life easier. I can easily take photos myself and if I take them myself, I can decide which pictures I am taking. If I want, my camera can also take pictures itself and it is a lot cheaper than Aibo. 3. Rich people might buy Aibo as an expensive toy which they can use to surprise their friends at parties. Perhaps people who live in flats in big cities are also attracted to Aibo because their living conditions are not suitable for a real dog. Maybe Aibo would be an attractive dog for very young children or old people because they don't have to take it for a walk or remember to feed it. It will probably never make a mess in the house or bite you, and I assume it won't become ill or die.

S. 15 **4b)** *(EH)* 1. a television: We use a television to watch and listen to different programmes. We can watch things like the news or different films. 2. a mobile: We use this phone to make and receive phone calls wherever we go. We can also use it to send messages, take photos, record voices or videos and to get into the internet. 3. an alarm (clock): We use it to wake us up in the mornings. 6. a laptop: This is a computer that we can take wherever we go because it is small and has a battery. We use it just like other computers. **5b)** *(EH)* 1. I phoned my mobile phone company to ask about the money they were asking me to pay for the month of June. A voice told me to wait for a few minutes and then some music played. Suddenly I heard a voice again and I thought someone was finally going to talk to me, but it was just another recorded voice which told me how wonderful the company was. Then I was told to wait for a few minutes again and the music came back. This went on for twenty minutes and in the end I gave up. I realized that it would be cheaper and more productive to go to town and visit the company myself! 2. I think this kind of telephone system is designed to help the companies, not the customers. If customers phone a company and the telephone is busy, they will call again later. But with this system, the customers wait because they think that someone will talk to them soon. In fact, all the customer is doing, is wasting time and money. This system is a big advantage for companies because it means that they do not have to employ a lot of people to answer the phone and connect customers to the right departments. It also means that the companies get a chance to talk about how wonderful their company is and it doesn't cost them a penny. Sometimes when you are phoning a company for help, they even make money from your phone call because you are charged more per minute for this service.

S. 16 **1c)** *(EH)* Judy says that she enjoys doing practical things and she would also like to work with people, especially children. She could work in health care, education or social work, for example as a nurse, a teacher or a charity worker. **2c)** *(EH)* 1. If you make a mistake you should try to correct it. 2. If we buy T-shirts for £5 and sell them for £10 we'll make a profit of one hundred percent. 3. I enjoy taking engines and other things apart in order to find out how they work. 4. Some companies sell their products at very low prices in order to gain an advantage over their competitors. 5. I always gain weight over Christmas because there are so many good things to eat. 6. My parents do most of their shopping online because it saves time. **2d)** *(EH)* 1. I'll make the coffee. 2. Can your mobile phone take photos? 3. I had breakfast early today. 4. Have you done your homework, yet?

S. 19 **1b)** *(EH)* 1. She is studying three subjects: Maths, Chemistry and Information Technology. 2. She has found them all interesting. 3. Yes, it does. 4. No, she isn't. She is thinking of doing Software Engineering. 5. Yes, she has. She did one at the end of year ten. 6. She supported the engineers who were developing solar energy technology at the time. 7. No, she didn't. She played a role in designing it. 8. They are developing an online learning program called the Virtual Classroom. 9. She won't be able to use it because she'll have left school by then. 10. No, she will be taking part in a sponsored bicycle ride. 11. She joined it seven months ago. 12. No, they haven't, but they will be having one soon. 13. No, she is looking forward to it.

S. 20 **4** *(EH)* 1. I hope I won't miss my bus. (*will future*) 2. I must hurry because my bus leaves in five minutes! (*simple present*) 3. I'm going to the doctor this afternoon. (*present progressive*) 4. I'm never going to watch Big Brother again. (*going-to future*) 5. I don't know what I'll be doing this time next year. (*future progressive*) 6. I put some bread out in the garden this evening. The birds will have eaten it by tomorrow morning. (*future perfect*)

S. 25 **2** 1. We want to raise money for old people. 2. I'm really looking forward to starting college. 3. I've been a member of a band for seven months. 4. I'm thinking of doing a work placement at the tax office. 5. My mother is a lawyer. 6. Can you lend me £200? 7. This cream is for sensitive skin. 8. We're leaving early tomorrow so we need to get up by 4 am. 9. This ice cream tastes delicious! 10. I would like to make things that I can sell. 11. Three years ago I took part in an exchange programme. 12. I speak fluent English/English fluently. 13. I'm afraid I can't come today. I'll come tomorrow. 14. This time tomorrow I will be lying on the beach!

S. 26 **2b)** "We'll miss the beginning of the film if we don't hurry. It starts at 8.30." 2. "I'll be taking my driving test." 3. "I'm going to buy Sam a DVD for his birthday." – "I'll help you to choose one." 4. "By next autumn I'll have left school. With a bit of luck I'll have started university."

S. 28 **5b)** *(EH)* I can't imagine life without my cell phone, and although I agree that it's important to have rules against using cell phones during lessons, I think it's wrong not to allow students to bring their phones to school at all. I need to be able to contact my mother as she often collects me after school. I have to be able to tell her if something happens that is going to make me late, for example, or if I feel ill and have to come home early.

S. 30 **2** *(EH)* **tactful:** John notices that his friend Paul seems unhappy about something. He waits until they are alone together and then asks him if there's anything the matter, or if he can help at all. John is very tactful. **sympathetic:** Emma got a bad grade in the last French test and is feeling upset. Her friend Fiona says how sorry she is and tells Emma that she understands how she feels. Fiona also talks about her own bad grades in Maths. She is very sympathetic. **reliable:** If Jack has arranged to meet his mates at a certain time, he always comes. If something happens that prevents him, he calls and explains why he can't be there. He's a really reliable person. **honest:** Jenny and Lucy are trying on clothes in a new shop. Jenny wants to buy a bright pink dress, but Lucy feels sure the colour doesn't suit Jenny! She tells her friend what she thinks – even if she knows Jenny will be disappointed. Lucy is very honest. **fun to be with:** Daisy is a great friend to have. She calls Liz and suggests spending Saturday morning in town. Liz feels great with Daisy because Daisy laughs a lot and always sees the funny side of things. Liz has a really happy time because Daisy is such fun to be with.

S. 31 **1** *(EH)* 1. I'm always buying things like hamburgers and chips. 2. He's always telling people how brilliant he is! 3. She's always buying things like earrings or lipsticks! 4. They're always saying I should work harder! 5. I'm always playing football or computer games! 6. He's always giving us so much homework! **3b)** *(EH)* 1. "So have I. I can watch all the programmes I like!/ But I haven't. We've only got a TV in the living room." 2. "So do mine. They're never at home when I get back from school./ My father does, but my mother only works two days a week." 3. "Neither can mine. She never learnt French at school./Mine can. She studied French at university!" 4. "So do we. But I don't like fish much actually./We never do. Nobody in our family likes fish!" 5. "So would I! When I leave school, I never want to go back – even as a teacher!/I wouldn't! I'd enjoy teaching sports for example." 6. "Nor do we. Last year we didn't go away at all!/But we do. We went to California last summer!" 7. "So does mine. He takes me with him on his way to work./Mine doesn't. He usually cycles to work." 8. "Nor do I! I spend it all far too quickly!/I do. My parents are actually quite generous."

S. 33 **1a)** *(EH)* They let him have parties at home. They didn't make him tidy his room regularly. They didn't make him do jobs in the house or garden. They didn't let him smoke in the house, but they let him watch TV as long as he liked. They made him say where he was going and when he would be back. They let him camp or spend weekends away with friends. **1b)** *(EH)* They certainly won't let him have any more parties at home! They probably will make him tidy his room. Perhaps they'll make him do jobs in the house or garden. Of course, they still won't let him smoke in the house. Maybe they won't always let him watch TV as long as he likes. They'll still expect him to say where he's going and when he'll be back. Perhaps they won't always let him camp or spend weekends away with friends. **2** *(EH)* 1. I'll let you know when my train arrives. 2. That made me realize how important friends are. 3. It made me laugh a lot, too. 4. It makes you wonder where she gets the money. 5. Don't let it worry you too much. 6. Let them think what they like.

S. 34 **5b)** *(EH)* 1. If you are long-sighted, you can see things that are far away more clearly than things that are near you. 2. Someone who is heavy-handed doesn't deal with people very tactfully. 3. If you catch someone red-handed, you discover them while they are doing something wrong.

S. 35 **1a)** *(EH)* 1. (She) feels she isn't accepted because she's different. 2. (They) haven't enough money (to buy her fashionable clothes). 3. (He) is out of work and only gets a little money from the government. 4. a lot of girls 5. (It) has been used a lot and shows signs of damage. 6. (I) was wanting and planning to buy (something). 7. (She) never thought I might have done it. 8. (I) am not able to stop myself getting unhappy and worried.

S. 37 **1a)** *(EH)* Lesley, a 16-year-old girl, has run away from home, and has made her parents and younger sister very unhappy and worried. **1c)** *(EH)* 1. No, Lesley didn't have a good relationship with her parents. She often had arguments with them although Anna thought they hadn't been too serious. 2. When they discovered that she had taken her mother's money/cash card, her parents knew it was serious. 3. They feel very unhappy and even blame themselves for not understanding their daughter better. They wonder whether they should have treated her differently. 4. They have looked for her in Glasgow and paid for posters. Lesley's mother has been to all the drug and youth advice centres, and at night they look round the town centre or go to concerts where they hope to find her. 5. Life at home has become more difficult for Anna. Her parents get upset very easily when they watch TV or when the phone rings. They are stricter with Anna than before, and they get very worried if she comes home a bit late. **2a)** *(EH)* **Mum:** tablets for depression; starts to cry; almost called the police. **Dad:** never seen (him) cry before; missed Lesley so much; scared it was his fault. **Both parents:** wondering: harder on her? softer on her?; blame themselves; spent nearly all money looking for Lesley; come home in tears; upset. **Anna:** (Lesley) done s.th. selfish and stupid; thanks to her, living with Mum and Dad hard; because of her, can't go out; (Anna) paying for what Lesley did; not looking forward to Christmas; please come home. **School friends:** Lesley: some kind of star; as if she'd done s.th. brave and exciting. **3a)** *(EH)* She ran away to Glasgow nine months ago, took some clothes and her mother's money. She had had arguments with her parents, but her sister hadn't taken them seriously. **3b)** *(EH)* What reasons might she have had? What were the arguments with her parents about? Did she run away alone? Was she in trouble of any kind? (Trouble with the police, perhaps? Was she in love? Was she expecting a baby? Was she taking drugs?) What happened to her after she got to Glasgow? **4b)** *(EH)* 1. When they get older, they don't want to spend time with their parents any more and want to do different things. They prefer to be with people of their own age. 2. She liked the hotel, but her parents were too strict and wanted her to be back early every evening. They had lots of arguments. 3. At that age you're too young to go to pubs or clubs, but you don't want your parents to tell you what to do. 4. Parents should plan holidays together with their children, so they can help to decide where to go. It's a big advantage to let them take a friend, too.

S. 38 **5** *(EH)* Most runaways are found/return home after just a few days. Half of all the people who are missing in Germany are children or young people. But only three percent stay away for longer than a year. In March 2006 there were 450 missing children, and 1,200 young people between 14 and 18. If parents are careful, their children won't feel the need to run away. They should talk to their children if they start to do badly at school or seem to have problems of any kind. Many children run away if they are unhappy at home or socially, and then get to know a new friend who is sympathetic. This is especially true when young people first fall in love, for example if a girl feels that her first boyfriend isn't accepted by her parents. This may make her want to run away. **6** *(EH)* Craig ist ein 16-jähriger Jugendlicher, der Probleme mit seinen Eltern hat. Er fühlt sich zu Unrecht ständig von ihnen kritisiert und findet, dass sie ihm zu viele Vorschriften machen. Deshalb schreibt er einen Brief an die Kummerkastentante Eve. Craig klagt, dass seine Eltern ihm vorschreiben, wann er seine Hausaufgaben machen, ins Bett gehen und Klavier üben soll. Er übt tatsächlich zu wenig, aber es motiviert ihn erst recht nicht, wenn sie ihm die ganze Zeit vorhalten, dass der Klavierunterricht viel Geld kostet. Außerdem drohen sie ihm, dass er als Arbeitsloser enden wird, wenn er nicht mehr für die Schule tut. Je mehr sie ihn kritisieren, desto genervter reagiert er und hört gar nicht mehr zu. Er versteht nicht, dass sie ihm vorwerfen, er sei unkommunikativ, denn er kommuniziert sehr gut mit seinen Freunden, meist über das Internet. Aber auch das ist seinen Eltern nicht recht. Sie finden, es sei Zeitverschwendung, dass er so viel Zeit am Rechner verbringt. Sie verstehen nicht, dass alle Jugendlichen heutzutage so kommunizieren. Er hat die Nase voll davon, dass er ständig als verwöhnt, undankbar und faul bezeichnet wird, und würde gerne wissen, was er tun kann, damit er besser mit seinen Eltern auskommt.

Eve, die Kummerkastentante, erklärt Craig zunächst, dass er mit seinen Problemen nicht alleine ist. Viele Teenager, die in der Pubertät mit körperlichen Veränderungen, Selbstfindung, dem Aufbau neuer Beziehungen und Prüfungsstress zu kämpfen haben, leiden unter Stimmungsschwankungen. Dies begründet die neuere wissenschaftliche Forschung mit dem Umbau von Strukturen im Gehirn. Weil die heutigen Eltern nicht mehr wissen, wie sie sich damals im selben Alter gefühlt haben, machen sie sich zu viele Sorgen. Sie führen die Veränderung auf ihr Versagen in der Erziehung zurück und versuchen strenger zu sein, was den Konflikt verschärft. Beide Seiten müssten versuchen, die Dinge entspannter zu sehen.

Eve schlägt Craig vor, dass er seinen Eltern doch etwas entgegenkommen solle. Schließlich wollten sie ja nur das Beste für ihn. Sie rät ihm zu mehr Offenheit. Er solle mit seinen Eltern über Gefühle reden, ihnen sagen, mit wem er über das Internet Kontakt hat, und sich ein bisschen mehr anstrengen. Dann würde sich das Verhältnis zu seinen Eltern bestimmt verbessern.

S. 39 **1a)** *(EH)* 1. ... and then last night it all became so bad that we had to start dealing with the problem. 2. ... she didn't accept because she thought it wasn't good enough for her. 3. Can you help me ...? 4. ... he's going to get strict and make me stop (staying out late). 5. ... try to get the waiter's attention by looking at him? 6. ... the expression on her face showed me that she didn't like the idea. **1b)** *(EH)* 1. My father can't sing at all – he has no ear for music. 2. She asked him to help her, but he didn't lift a finger. 3. We're going to get a new car. Our old one is on its last legs! **2)** *(EH)* 1. I just can't make them understand how I feel about things. 2. OK, let me help you with it. 3. Dad made me plant some new bushes and trees. 4. I think I'll have the food delivered by a party service/restaurant. 5. It didn't make us laugh at all. 6. Don't let it get cold.

S. 41 **1b)** *(EH)* 1. At Thanksgiving Americans remember the special meal the Pilgrims shared with the Native Americans in 1621. At first life in America was very hard for the Pilgrims and many people died. But the Native Americans showed the Pilgrims how to grow food and helped them to survive in their new country. 2. The Fourth of July is the anniversary of the Declaration of Independence in 1776. The thirteen colonies in the east had been ruled by Britain, but then they decided that they wanted to rule themselves. Now every year on this date Americans celebrate with parties, parades and fireworks. 3. Boston Harbour is where the Boston Tea Party took place in 1773. Britain had put a new tax on tea, and this made the colonists very angry. So a cargo of tea was thrown into the water. This protest was one of the events that led to the War of Independence. 4. The Spanish discovered America in 1492 and they were also the people who brought horses and cows to America. Cattle ranches became an important part of the development of the country. For many people the cowboy is still a symbol of America.

S. 43 **6a)** Make a fire in the highest place in the area. Hold a blanket over the fire to collect the smoke under it. Take the blanket away to allow some smoke to escape. Return the blanket to stop the smoke again. Repeat as often as necessary until the signal has been sent. **6b)** *(EH)* Find a dry, flat piece of wood and a stick. Make a point at one end of the stick. Then put the point on the flat piece of wood and turn the stick between your hands as fast as you can. Go on doing this until smoke starts to appear. Then blow the smoke carefully and add a few dry leaves. When the leaves are burning, start adding small sticks to increase the size of the fire. **7** *(EH)* 1. Britain had thirteen colonies on the east coast of America. 2. Britain was at war with France both in Europe and in America. 3. The links with Britain were originally an advantage for the colonies because they were protected by Britain and because they were able to trade with the mother country/Britain. 4. Britain introduced new taxes in the colonies. 5. A cargo of tea was thrown into Boston Harbour by the angry colonists. 6. The sight of British soldiers in the streets helped to give the people in the different colonies a sense of identity as Americans. 7. The date of the Declaration of Independence was 4th July 1776. 8. The American leader in the War of Independence was George Washington. 9. The African slaves had to work on plantations in the south. 10. The Native Americans were the first group of people to arrive in America. 11. The pioneers often camped in a circle at night so that they could defend themselves better if they were attacked by Native Americans. 12. Gold was found in California in 1848. 13. Lewis and Clark explored Louisiana, west of the Mississippi. 14. Sacajawea originally belonged to the Shoshone tribe. 15. Columbus first called Native Americans 'Indians' (because he thought he had arrived in India). 16. The Native Americans depended on the buffalo. 17. The Sioux won their famous victory against General Custer in the Battle of the Little Big Horn. 18. The name that was given to special pieces of land for Native Americans was 'reservations'.

S. 46 **3** 1. The Indians living on the Great Plains had a great love and respect for nature and everything belonging to the natural world. 2. They believed that all living things would return to the earth again in time. 3. This idea of the 'circle of life' leading from birth to death meant that the circle became an important symbol. 4. They saw this circle (or cycle) in the sun rising and going down again each day and in the changing seasons. 5. The tipis made by the women were circular, and there were often circular designs painted on the sides. 6. The beautifully decorated clothes worn for tribal festivals sometimes also showed a circle standing out as a religious symbol. 7. Almost all Indian tribes believed that a god called 'the Great Spirit' had created the whole of nature. 8. They thought that everything created on the earth was naturally dependent on everything else, and that there was a spirit hidden deep in every animal, every mountain, every river. **4b)** *(EH)* 1. Cowboys did not want to get into trouble while they were riding because they had to take their cattle a long way up north to the rail stations. They had no reason to dislike Indians or to want to fight against them. Cowboys worked in teams. Sometimes there were up to 5,000 animals. They worked very long hours and were in the saddle all day. If they met Indians, they usually traded with them, as they needed food on their journey. 2. Native Americans were useful members of a team of cowboys because they were very good with horses, they were tough, and they knew the country well. If the team crossed an Indian reservation they could sometimes help by interpreting, at least if the Indians there spoke a language they understood.

S. 49 **1** *(EH)* The first settlers crossed the Great Plains quickly, because the land they saw did not seem at all good for farming, so naturally they did not want to live there. During the 1850s and 1860s, however, this attitude gradually began to change. Wanting to attract new settlers, the railroad companies advertised land which they sold cheaply, and in 1862 the US government even decided to give land away! If settlers agreed to build a house and live there for five years, they were allowed 160 acres of land free. The government made 2.5 million acres available in this way. The first homesteaders travelled west in wagons, but as soon as the railroads were built, people began to come by train. Most of the people that settled came as families. They were full of hope when they arrived on the Plains, having read all the wonderful adverts. Farmers that came from the eastern states had brought their own seeds and farming tools. But when they started to work, they got a terrible shock because their seeds did not grow and the tools they had brought with them were not suitable for the land there. These were their main problems: The weather was often very windy, but it got terribly hot in the summer months. In winter there were sometimes awful snow storms, and later in the year heavy rain was often followed by many weeks of dry weather. Then there were often fires which were spread by the wind and which could ruin all the crops in a short time. There was no wood for building fences, so wild animals or cattle were able to get into the fields and ruin the crops. And as there were very few trees on the Plains, the settlers' homes had to be built out of dried earth. There was simply not enough water for wheat to grow, and the hard earth was a problem because it was so difficult to plough. On top of all this, there were sometimes millions of grasshoppers that came and ate all the crops in just a few hours. Life on the Plains was hard, especially because it was impossible to keep the houses clean. They became dusty in the dry weather, and very wet when it rained. Of course, there were no toilets or clean water, and this meant that illness was caused by the dirty conditions people had to live in. There were also few doctors to treat people when they were sick, and children often died of diseases. Not surprisingly, having a baby was a dangerous event in women's lives, and many died in childbirth. **2b)** *(EH)* 2. This is absolutely untrue! 5. I must point out that … 6. What facts does … actually know about … ?/Has … got any real facts about this? 7. It is simply not right to say that … 8. (can't be rewritten politely) 12. I don't agree with that article on … at all.

S. 50 **1b)** *(EH)* 2. Mary's teacher thought the ritual was a positive thing, partly because it was a chance for girls to compete on equal terms with boys. 6. Ernie thought that the ritual was a crazy idea. Mary had thought so, too, at first, but when she heard this, she felt angry and began to realize that there were good reasons behind it. 8. Mary's grandfather hadn't eaten the berries because he had found a dead deer on the first day and was able to eat its meat during his Ta-Na-E-Ka. **2** *(EH)* When Roger left Mary, he walked through the forest, looking at the birds in the trees and feeling happy and full of confidence. He was sure he would manage the endurance test well. But when he woke up on the second morning, under his pile of leaves, he felt cold and hungry. The orange berries his grandfather had shown him tasted terrible! The next day, feeling awfully hungry, he tried again and again to catch a grasshopper, and in the end he was successful. But it tasted so terrible that he had to be sick on the grass. He felt so bad then that he thought he might even die! The weather was really wet on the fourth day, and by this time Roger's feet were a mass of blisters, and the pain was hard to bear. When he lay down to sleep that evening, he was glad it was the last night of the test. The next day, Roger arrived back home and his grandfather was standing at the door, welcoming him. Although it had been such an awful experience, Roger felt proud that he had come through it successfully.

S. 52 **6b)** *(EH)* 1. Julia hat sie erwähnt, weil Lewis und Clark damals durch das Land der Nez Perce gereist sind, und die Indianer haben sie sehr herzlich empfangen/als ganz besondere

Gäste behandelt. 2. Die Weißen hatten versprochen, dass sie sich in dem Gebiet der Nez Perce nicht niederlassen würden. Im Jahr 1877 wurde aber genau dort in den Bergen Gold entdeckt. 3. Als die Nez Perce auf dem Weg zu einem Reservat waren, gab es Ärger mit weißen Siedlern. Die Indianer gingen auf den Kriegspfad und einige Weiße wurden getötet. 4. Viele von ihnen waren krank und sehr schwach, deshalb mussten sie kurz vor der Grenze Rast machen. Dort wurden sie dann von den US Soldaten geschlagen. 5. Die Nez Perce kamen in ein Reservat, aber Joseph wurde von seinen Leuten getrennt und musste in ein anderes Reservat. Dort blieb er dann bis zu seinem Tod.

S. 53 **2** 1. A stagecoach in the west travelled for up to fifteen hours a day, making journeys of 40 to 60 miles in the summer months. 2. In hundreds of cowboy films, stagecoaches crossing the dusty western landscape are stopped by outlaws or Indians. 3. In reality, the stagecoaches used in the west had little to do with the lives of cowboys. 4. However, knowing passengers usually had money or valuable goods with them, outlaws did attack stagecoaches quite often. 5. In 1877, the coaches belonging to the Wells Fargo company were attacked 200 times in a single month! 6. But soon the railroads built across the continent put an end to the days of stagecoach travel, making journeys quicker, safer and more comfortable.

S. 56 **5b)** *(EH)* I would sometimes buy Fair Trade products, although they are more expensive, because I think it is important to help farmers and workers in developing countries and to try to make sure they are paid fairly for the things they produce. Of course, there are sometimes cases where owners of big Fair Trade plantations don't pay their workers as much as they should, and that's very unfair. But in most cases, I expect the Fair Trade system does help a lot of people. There are still poor farmers in lots of countries that do not receive any help, but I hope that if more people buy Fair Trade products, the system will gradually spread to more and more parts of the world. **6** *(EH)* Arthur Winston, an American from Los Angeles, retired from work on his hundredth birthday, after 72 years. His job was looking after buses and cleaning them. He only missed work once, when his wife died in 1988. He never smoked or drank alcohol, and he thinks this is the reason for his long healthy life. In 1996 President Clinton made him 'worker of the year'. He had actually wanted to be a mechanic, but because of the colour of his skin he was not given a chance. This was in the 1930s. In his first job as a caretaker in 1924, he earned 41 cents an hour.

S. 58 **1b)** *(EH)* What is Silicon Valley famous for? Who discovered California in 1542? When did California become part of the US? What is Lassen Peak? What kind of tree is the General Sherman? What is the capital of California? Which part of LA do many big stars live in? Give three examples of leading industries in California. What is Yosemite? What is Death Valley?

S. 59 **2c)** *(EH)* Inventions lead to new industries that develop new products. This creates jobs in the area. Then people have more money to spend. At the same time these new industries attract connected industries which also create jobs. Because people have more money to spend, there is an increase in new shops and services in the area. This means it becomes a popular area to live, and so new people arrive. The effect of this is even more growth. New people bring new ideas with them that can lead to more new inventions. As a result, the circle of success continues and increases. **3a)** *(EH)* San Francisco and Los Angeles both have a warm climate, with the warmest months in the summer. However, Los Angeles is always warmer than San Francisco, and is also considerably drier.

S. 60 **2** *(EH)* 1. Agriculture, which most of the state's wealth comes from/from which most of the state's wealth comes, is a leading industry in California. 2. Many people who/that work in this part of the economy grow fruit and vegetables. 3. California usually has the kind of warm and sunny weather which/that farmers want. 4. The state produces many wines, whose quality is among the best in the world. 5. Other farmers whose products are not crops also make a contribution to the economy. 6. The farms provide many jobs for workers whose families need the money. 7. The San Joaquin Valley, which lies between San Francisco and Los Angeles, is the largest dairy region in the world. 8. But some people are not happy about the dairy farms which/that they have to live near/near which they have to live. 9. The cows, which each produce 19.3 pounds of gases a year, pollute the air. 10. Smog, which is bad enough in Los Angeles, is even worse in parts of the San Joaquin Valley!

S. 61 **4b)** *(EH)* 1. He is very good at his job. 2. I am waiting for a reply to my application. 3. Are you interested in learning another language? 4. They are not afraid of hard work. 5. It's interesting to find out what people spend their money on. 6. All children should have a right to a good education.

S. 62 **2a)** *(EH)* 1. I noticed her get off a bus and go into a health food store. 2. I saw him grab a photographer's camera and throw it into the bushes, and I heard him laugh while he was doing it! 3. I saw her buy ice creams and give them to her children. 4. I heard him complaining about the food/his meal. 5. I saw her coming out of an expensive store with her little dog/carrying a little dog out of an expensive store. 6. I watched him jogging/running in a park.

S. 63 **3b)** *(EH)* 1. Last year I went on a trip to learn about survival in the wilderness. 2. Every night I had to make a shelter for protection against the weather. 3. One day I was given a shock by the appearance of a big bear in front of me. 4. Another day I slipped on some rocks, but luckily the fall didn't cause an injury. 5. I'm proud of my achievement and I also feel I have a much better understanding of nature now. **3c)** *(EH)* 1. Our modern lifestyle creates a lot of pollution. 2. The development of national parks has helped to protect beautiful places. 3. The next meeting of our environmental group is on Friday. 4. She expressed her annoyance very clearly. 5. The removal of trees from hills causes landslides. 6. The discovery of a rare plant in the forest was very exciting. **4b)** *(EH)* 1. Ruhe und Frieden 2. sauber und ordentlich 3. hier und dort/da 4. ab und zu/von Zeit zu Zeit/gelegentlich 5. überall 6. gründlich satt haben/überhaben/die Nase voll haben

S. 64 **6** *(EH)* Seid nicht achtlos gegenüber Bären! In Yosemite müssen jedes Jahr Schwarzbären getötet werden, als direkte Folge der Achtlosigkeit von Menschen. Die Rede ist von einem Bärenproblem, aber die Bären tragen keine Schuld. Aufgrund ihres starken Geruchssinns werden Schwarzbären von menschlicher Nahrung angelockt. Haben Bären einmal von diesen Nahrungsmitteln gegessen, dann suchen sie immer wieder danach – in Rucksäcken, auf Picknicktischen und sogar in den Autos der Parkbesucher. Die natürliche Angst der Bären vor Menschen lässt nach und sie können aggressiv werden. Wenn sie zu aggressiv werden, müssen sie oft getötet werden. Die einzige Möglichkeit das zu verhindern, besteht darin sämtliche Nahrungsmittel gut zu verstauen.

S. 65 **1b)** *(EH)* The verb 'wipe (away)' can mean both 'clean' and 'destroy'. So 'stop wiping away ancient forests' has a double meaning. It refers to using toilet paper which is made from the forest, and also refers to the danger of destroying the forest.

S. 66 **2b)** *(EH)* Do you still have relatives in Austria/Europe? At what age did you leave school? Which of your movies do you like best? Did you take drugs to help with your bodybuilding? What issues do you think are most important in California? Would you like to become President one day?

S. 69 **1b)** *(EH)* 1. On Sam's sixteenth birthday he discovers that he can travel into the future, where he meets himself as an old man. 2. Sam can only travel into the future when it's a full moon. 3. She got the idea from a dream. 4. She uses the image of a tree which grew and had fruit, and with branches she needed to cut off. 5. Read a lot. Write about things that interest you. Write in your own style/voice. Never give up. 6. She likes the recognition, being praised and knowing that people enjoy her novel. She finds the attention too much some times. She doesn't like being asked for her autograph, signing copies of her book or getting fan letters from strange people. **2a)** *(EH)* The author probably felt